MONA LISA'S MOUSTACHE

Making Sense of a Dissolving World

MARY SETTEGAST

Mona Lisa's Moustache

MONA LISA'S MOUSTACHE

Making Sense of a Dissolving World

Mary Settegast

PHANES PRESS
An Alexandria Book

An Alexandria Book

Alexandria Books explore intersections—the meeting points between culture, philosophy, myth, and the creative spirit. *www.cosmopolis.com*

Published by Phanes Press, P.O. Box 6114, Grand Rapids, MI 49516 USA
www.phanes.com

Library of Congress Cataloging in Publication Data

Settegast, Mary.
    Mona Lisa's moustache : making sense of a dissolving world / Mary Settegast
        p. cm. — (An Alexandria book)
    Includes bibliographical references and index.
    ISBN 1-890482-90-0
    1. Civilization, Modern—1950—Philosophy. 2. Form (Aesthetics) 3. Art,
Modern—20th century—Philosophy. 4. Postmodernism. 5. Pluralism.
6. Relativity. I. Title. II. Series.

CB430 .S475 2001
306'.09'04—dc21
                                                                00-58909

This book is printed on alkaline paper that conforms to the permanent paper standard developed by the National Information Standards Organization.

Printed and bound in the United States of America
on recycled paper by Johnson Printing.

Contents

Illustrations

Acknowledgments

My main indebtedness is to my observers, the authors named in the bibliography, whose ideas and words are the life of this essay. To the artists, museums, and galleries who provided transparencies of the works reproduced here goes another set of thanks, which extends to the photographers who created the reproductions and the heirs, estates, and artists themselves who gave permission to use their work.

I want to thank my editor, Alice Levine, for her scrupulous assistance in polishing the manuscript, and the several people who gave it critical readings at one stage or another: John Carney, Suzanne Walker, Loftin Elvey, Morris Fry, John David Ebert, William Irwin Thompson, and Naomi Lucks. The suggestions made by each of you were essential to the improvement of the text, and I am very grateful.

Those who put the book together, and put up with the author's eccentricities, deserve special praise. David Fideler proved himself an ideal publisher in every way. Mira Perrizo, a true wonder-woman, guided the process of assembling and coordinating the material for printing. Her equally amazing spouse, Scott Perrizo, did a magnificent job of page layouts and interior design, and the combined efforts of Debra Topping, Melanie Walker, and Chris Dyson brought forth a peerless book jacket.

Finally I owe thanks to the family and friends who were always available to hear me out, urge me on, laugh and cry on cue, and cook and garden for me through the life of this project. Sybil Settegast and Carol Kobb, Thea Tenenbaum and Raffaele Malferrari, Suzanne Walker, George Peters and Melanie Walker, Ginny Threefoot, Isa Catto, and Sara Licht excel at every sort of sustenance.

For Emiliano, Gelsey, and Michael

FIGURE 1.
Georges Braque,
Piano and Mandola,
Winter 1909–1910.

I

The Search for Pattern

Shortly before her death, Dame Rebecca West was asked to name the dominant mood of our time. "A desperate search for a pattern," was her reply. The ninety-year-old writer may have been speaking for her generation alone. That exchange took place in the early 1980s, and today the dominant mood feels something more like a search for venture capital. But sooner or later, for each of us, the question of pattern, of meaning, is bound to come up.

And there is still no pattern in sight. Or rather, there is no *one* pattern, no one universally meaningful way of looking at things that would make sense of today's world. What we have instead are a great many different beliefs about the meaning of this time, including the overriding and very well-developed belief that there is no meaning. We also have the sense that we must choose between beliefs. Along with the many other choices we are asked to make today, we feel that we must choose what, if anything, we think the world is about.

Faced with this situation, some have chosen to retreat into realms of the fundamentally bizarre. In the confused and conflicted "hothouse atmosphere" of the late twentieth century, a crazy explanation has seemed to many people better than no explanation at all. As one cultural historian observes, at least part of the reason people so desperately want to believe in alien visitations is that they no longer understand their fellow human beings or the situations they find themselves in: "These people want something to be happening out there."⁷²

Others have chosen the security offered by groups that claim to represent the one infallible and unerring truth, a position known as inerrantism, or literalism, and today usually associated with belief in the literal truth of the Bible. Critics point out that inerrantism is actually a counterrevolution: a rebellion against the complexity of contemporary life, the constant battles among different groups with different views of reality, the incessant demands on the individual to make choices. The inerrantists are, in the words of an observer, "in hot pursuit of a civilization with no uncertainties."³

The same may be said of less openly declared forms of fundamentalism. Most of the single-minded groups of our time, from Marxist intellectuals to scientific technocrats to New Age transcendentalists, believe that they alone have the answer, which leaves them little to say to one another. "Indeed, from a millenarian point of view," notes a critic, "all one can do is preach. To listen to one's opponents is to listen only to falsehood."²⁶ We have all experienced conversation with someone who subscribes to a handed-down point of view. The predictability of his responses is frustrating, boring, and ultimately saddening. How might he have added to my understanding of the world if he had chosen to see it with his own eyes?

Perhaps he is thinking the same thing. It is easy to perceive the fundamentalism of others but difficult to see one's own. Christians tend to criticize Muslim fundamentalism without recognizing their own conformity; capitalists who criticize the rigidity of socialism forget that the fundamentalism of the free market is no less fixed.[80] Even when our worldview has nothing to do with religious faith, we tend to endow it with the kind of absolute certainty that was once universally provided by the church.

But absolute certainties were contradicted by twentieth-century realities, and those who want to live fully in their own time have chosen not to seek safe havens but to accept—even appreciate—the fact that nothing today is "given" except the ability to question and observe. To follow a received doctrine of any kind, including the doctrine of no-meaning sponsored by Western science, has begun to feel uncomfortable if not unnatural for an increasing number of individuals. Rather than search for a universal pattern, they have chosen to put together their own ways of looking at the world. Some of their efforts, especially those that are exclusively self-absorbed, seem outrageous, but others are more inclusive and take advantage of what this particular time has to offer. The most ambitious of these attempts and, I believe, the most productive are those that try to see the world from all sides as well as inside out, an undertaking that only became possible in the twentieth century.

This evident "age of meaninglessness"[148] was marked by an explosion of information, and however overwhelmed some of us felt (and feel) by the amount of "data" now being flashed around the globe, it has given us access to the worldviews of all times and all places. Contemporary historians and archaeologists have collapsed time, bringing the known perspectives of past epochs into our awareness. Ethnographers and anthropologists have compressed space, presenting to us the reality models of contemporary peoples everywhere. How others once saw and now see the world not only reveals the limitations of the Western scientific perspective but encourages us to go beyond them.

In fact, in the absence of a given belief system, we may now be able to approach truth, or construct a working reality for ourselves, *only* by looking at the world from more than one point of view. This book explores that premise. The following chapter describes what seems to be one of the defining qualities of our time: the dissolution of form — by which I mean the disintegration of boundaries, values, conventions, all formal rules that once contained the arts, and most of our habitual ways of perceiving the world. Each of the remaining chapters then looks at the meaning of this breakdown from a different perspective, moving from limited and essentially pessimistic to larger and more subtle points of view. In other words, things get better as we go along, seeing the breakdown as the result of (1) global consumer capitalism, (2) environmental deterioration, (3) the end of a cycle of time, (4) the beginning of a new cycle, (5) a shift in the evolution of human consciousness, and finally, (6) seeing the dissolution of form as a cause for celebration.

These several ways of looking at our time are not intended to be compared or shopped by those seeking a finished worldview to believe in, those searching for a single pattern. The point is not to choose between them but to hold all perspectives at once. The twentieth century gave us evidence, in physics and mathematics, that reality is too complex and plural to fit within any one theoretical description. The absence today of an agreed-upon worldview might therefore suggest that the pattern we seek is in fact *patterns,* and that other ways of looking at the world can add depth and nuance to our original understanding. The early twentieth century Cubist painters were among the first to recognize the error in a single point of view (figures 1 and 2). Like Braque and Picasso, we will be trying in these pages to portray our subject from all sides in hopes of capturing it whole.

FIGURE 2. Pablo Picasso, *Portrait of Daniel-Henry Kahnweiler,* 1910.

2

The Dissolution of Form

The collapse of the atom was equated, in my soul, with the collapse of the whole world. Suddenly, the stoutest walls crumbled. Everything became uncertain, precarious and insubstantial.
—Wassily Kandinsky, *Rückblicke*, 1913
(after the discovery of the electron
at the end of the nineteenth century)

Things fall apart …
—W.B. Yeats, *The Second Coming*, 1920

If we accept the idea that nothing is given except the ability to question and observe, a logical first question might be: what's happening? Or what seem to be the significant events and qualities of our time? And second: what, if anything, does that mean? Can I make any sense for myself out of the seemingly random events of today's world?

Leaving the sense-making question for later, let's ask first what's happening. What are the distinguishing characteristics of our world? The collapsing of time has already been named. Not only has the past been brought into the present, but time itself, and therefore change, seems to have speeded up. The compressing of space was also mentioned earlier, a phenomenon that appears to be leading to the globalization of human culture. These two events—the collapse of our traditional notions of time and space—are basic to a single quality that seems to dominate our time: the disintegration, or dissolution, of form.

Breakdowns of structure are everywhere to be observed: in social and moral codes, in gender distinctions, in literature, music, architecture and painting, in politics, economics, and personal relationships. There is no longer an absolute, a "proper" form, anywhere. If we're not yet at a place where *anything* goes, we seem to be very close.

The process of disintegration began early in the twentieth century with physicists demonstrating that what we regard as reality, the image of the world revealed to us by our perceptions, is an illusion. Solid matter was dissolved into fields of energy; hard discrete objects were replaced with dynamic processes; matter and energy became interchangeable. With the discovery of the indeterminacy, or uncertainty, principle, the so-called laws of physics were converted into statements about relative instead of absolute certainties. Thus began a process of "thorough and relentless uncertainization"[12] that is still going on.

What once was separate and distinct is no longer so. Nineteenth-century physics was all about the discreteness of things and how their constituent parts influence one another across that separation. In the twentieth century, applying the principles of quantum physics to the world around us has led to the conclusion that the world of objects cannot be separated from the observing subject, that "scientific observation and explanation cannot proceed without affecting the nature of the object observed."[149] When even the traditional dualities of world versus man, object versus subject, turn out to be untenable from the standpoint of physics, it seems clear that we not only influence, but in some measure create, our reality.

We are further informed that time and space, the physicist's raw materials, have been dissolved and are no longer to be viewed as separate, independent entities. "Space, which had been considered timeless, is actually inseparable from motion, which involves time."[161] Space and time are hereafter one, and the familiar time and space that order our daily experience, though concretely measurable, are now described as "shams, pure conventions."[159] Even as we struggle with the concept of a four-dimensional space-time continuum, our everyday perception is that time itself has accelerated while space has shrunk. The pace of life seems to be racing, and the entire geographical world is suddenly "here" as the barriers of conventional space are overcome by telecommunications technology.

The rapidity of change is so extreme that some observers question whether late-twentieth-century humans are not somehow different than people who lived a thousand — or even a hundred — years ago. We are certainly a lot less sure of what our lives are about. The indeterminacy, or uncertainty, that characterizes the subatomic world of quantum physics now pervades Western society. It is widely accepted that representations of reality in the West, the stories we used to tell ourselves about the world and our place in it, can no longer be taken as truth. Even Western science is now seen as another form of socially constructed reality and "not a secret technique for taking objective photographs of the universe."[3]

Cultural historians have borrowed the term indeterminacy from physicists to describe tendencies in our society toward heterodoxy, pluralism, eclecticism, randomness, and especially, "deformation," a word that includes, according to one scholar:

> a dozen current terms of unmaking: decreation, disintegration, deconstruction, decenterment, displacement, difference, discontinuity, disjunction, disappearance, decomposition, de-definition, demystification, detotalization, delegitimation.[58]

All of these tendencies have been pronounced typical of the late twentieth century, defining in fact what is meant by the term *postmodern,* and all signify the breakdown of established forms. As described by a sociologist, postmodernism is "the culture that takes seriously the breaking apart of the world."[83]

Elsewhere in the academic world, scholars have concluded that meaning in literature derives only from the relationships between the words themselves—that there is, in some sense, "nothing outside of the text." Loss of confidence in the ability to reflect reality in a literary context is further complicated by the suspicion that language does not merely represent reality but actually constitutes it. Where language was once regarded as a medium that describes the real world, postmodern theorists tend to see it as a medium that *creates* the real world.[5]

A more playful approach was taken by postmodern breakdowns of form in the arts, beginning in the 1960s with the pop art of Andy Warhol and Tom Wesselmann (figure 3), Robert Venturi's decorated sheds and pop buildings, John

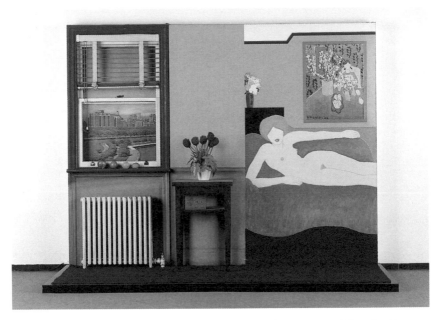

FIGURE 3. Tom Wesselmann, *Great American Nude #48*, 1963. Oil and collage on canvas, acrylic and collage on board, enameled radiator, table, pot of flowers, window assemblage, c. 84 x 108 x 34 inches.

Cage's silent music (*4'33"* was actually first performed in 1952), and the wildly experimental activities of the Judson Dance Theater. Any attempt to pin down a definable form in the arts was consistently undermined by the unpredictable and utterly irreverent attitudes of these artists toward the conventions of time, space, and tradition. The distinction between high culture and so-called mass, or popular, culture continued to dissolve through the 1980s and 1990s, as did the boundaries between categories of art. Today's art world is still characterized by "the exuberant use of all modes to

FIGURE 4. *Lampwick's Dilemma,* David Salle, 1989. Oil and acrylic on canvas with insert panels, 94 x 136 inches.

explode any and all definitions of genre."[18] With virtually no restrictions on methods or materials, a kind of wacky eclecticism continues to mock any attempt to distinguish between formal categories.

Conventional distinctions between past and present have also been dissolved. In postmodern art the tendency to incorporate elements and styles from the past, often playfully, overwhelmed the formal boundaries of time, as seen in David Salle's *Dilemma* (figure 4). Old and new styles were mixed together with irony, whimsy, and an over-the-top use of parody and pastiche. As one critic described postmodern painting:

> The past pokes through the fabric of time to lie side by side with the present, and the future, too. Academic disciplines cross over the hidden barriers supposedly separating them: history with myth. The canvas churns with funny, endearing, often horrifying depictions, placed in highly charged juxtapositions. The seemingly ugly and the accepted-as-beautiful meet at every moment, and try as we may we cannot keep them apart.[39]

More significant, perhaps, is the breakdown of distinctions between art and nonart or, as accomplished in performance art, distinctions between art and life. In a recent survey the people most likely to know were asked, "What is art?" All answered with some variation of the idea that more or less anything can be designated as art or that art is just whatever people say it is.[98]

In what some see as "the deterioration of the traditional narrative,"[46] late-twentieth-century writers of fiction began producing novels in which past and present, history and fiction, street slang and elaborately literary language were juxtaposed without warning onto the page. Architects as well began tossing together styles from different periods; in contrast to modern architecture, the postmodern did not reject tradition but included it in "an often ironical recycling of what is usable as decorum."[4] Philip Johnson's famous AT&T (now Sony) building in New York City features a Chippendale flourish on the pediment, Greco-Roman columns at the base, and a Byzantine arch over the entrance of an otherwise state-of-the-art modern skyscraper. In his Piazza d'Italia (figure 5), Charles Moore constructed a fountain enclosed by a colonnade of the five "Italian" orders of architecture, creating a playful blend of water and neon with canonic proportions of stainless steel and marble finish.[66]

This tendency to collapse time, to fuse elements from the sometimes-not-so-distant past, is clearly visible in postmodern dance, described by Twyla Tharp as "everything that came before, *plus!*"[151] The once-rigid barrier between ballet and modern dance, already weakened in the 1950s, has been dissolving since the 1960s, as has the definition of dance itself. As one critic remarked of the work of a leading contemporary choreographer: "There is no *way* to make a dance; there is no kind of movement that can't be included in these dances; there is no kind of sound that is not proper for accompaniment."[71]

In classical music, traditional concepts of space and time gave way at the beginning of the twentieth century, and a world of musical predictability went with them. Postmodern composers, building largely on the midcentury work of John Cage, then took the earlier breakdowns of form into unimagined realms where the traditional musical building blocks — melody, harmony, rhythm — were of far less interest than the inventive possibilities of such sounds as brain waves, birdcalls, magnets, ostrich eggs, and electronic devices, occasionally accompanied by conventional instruments.[76] Elements of chance and wit, inventiveness and improvisation, are as prominent here as in contemporary literature and dance, and lead again to the question: what is music?

In the pop music culture of MTV, the breakdown of narrative rationality is carried to its most disjointed extreme. The

FIGURE 5. Charles W. Moore, Piazza d'Italia, New Orleans, 1976–1979. Photograph courtesy of Norman McGrath.

viewer is bombarded with rapid-fire images that seem to have little relation to each other and no objective meaning. In the words of one critic, "MTV refuses any clear recognition of previously sacred aesthetic boundaries; images from German Expressionism, French Surrealism, and Dadaism ... are mixed together with those pillaged from the noir, gangster, and horror films in such a way as to obliterate differences."[46]

Blurring of boundaries permeates the media as well; distinctions are hard to find today between high journalism and low ("the mainstream press has gone from scoffing at the tabloids to invading their turf"),[96] between TV content and TV commercials, and between news and entertainment ("news, public affairs, and history itself are morphing into entertainment").[2] Journalistic content experienced a similar breakdown of taboos. Watching the press briefings as the Monica Lewinsky story unfolded, one reporter remarked: "You get the idea that nothing is sacred after all. Nothing is out of the arena of discussion."[24]

In the world of commerce, the disintegration of time-space restrictions has given us an international economy in which companies operate in a twenty-four-hour world, national boundaries are irrelevant, and jobs are networked around the world via computer. This unbounded world seems to one observer "simultaneously so blithely interconnected and so completely out of control."[73] An increasingly integrated global economy may seem to run counter to the contemporary trend toward decentering and dissolution of form, but actually it does not. Even before the financial crises overseas in the late 1990s, an analyst observed: "The global system has no center. It is a decentered space of flows rather than a clearly hierarchically structured space of production."[18] When the stabilizers that were imposed by the post–World War II nation states broke down in the 1990s, Western governments allowed the world market to expand without limit, hoping that its equilibrium would be maintained by faster growth.

The long-term wisdom of this approach is uncertain, but the dissolving of economic regulations—the global market version of "anything goes"—will undoubtedly mean further disintegration in the earth's own natural order. Threatened environments and species, worldwide pollution, even the possible breakdown of established patterns of the earth's climate attest to the excesses of industrial activity in the twentieth century. A concerned observer concludes: "In this disintegrating phase of our industrial civilization, we now see ourselves not as the splendor of creation, but as the most pernicious mode of earthly being. ... If there were a parliament of creatures, its first decision might well be to vote the humans out of the community, too deadly a presence to tolerate any further."[17]

Not all, or even most, Americans share that perception, nor are there guarantees that future generations will notice the disintegration of the natural world. It has been argued that we are already abandoning nature by constructing theme-park simulations of natural environments that seek to improve on the real. Indeed, some critics maintain that synthetic settings and surrogate experience are becoming the preferred American way of life: environment as entertainment and artifice, the theme park as the country's biggest growth industry. The breakdown of distinctions between the real and the fake is most visibly celebrated in places like

Las Vegas, where a hotel and casino complex such as Bellagio boasts an eight-acre "Lake Como" surrounded by transplanted Italian trees. In the words of an authoritative critic: "Built to be exactly what it is, Las Vegas is the real, real fake at the highest, loudest and most authentically inauthentic level of illusion."[63] It is a virtual reality.

And what today is not? To go back to the opening of this chapter, the most radical dissolution of form in the twentieth century seems to be the collapse of our accustomed notion of reality. We have become increasingly convinced that all worldviews are socially constructed and that official versions of reality—versions set forth by churches, politicians, scientists, artists, and the news media—are human inventions.[64] This uncertainty about the true nature of the world contributes to the confusion surrounding the term "virtual reality." Seeming to apply alternately to everything and nothing, the virtual reality label can theoretically be attached to every representational image or simulation, from photographs and television to theme parks and Vegas hotels.

The increasing lack of distinction between the virtual and the real is celebrated enthusiastically by those involved in the field of electronic simulation, the Virtual Reality that identifies itself as such. These innovators claim that our most basic ideas of reality will be redefined when we electronically surround ourselves (by putting on a headset or walking into a media room) with a responsive and accurate simulation of real experience. According to one of the main players: "VR vividly demonstrates that our social contract with our own tools has brought us to a point where *we have to decide fairly soon what it is we as humans ought to be-*

come, because we are on the brink of having the power of creating any experience we desire."[117]

One wonders how it is possible to decide what we as humans ought to become when we are increasingly uncertain about what we are. In an indeterminate world, a world without agreed-upon standards of behavior, each individual has only himself as the ultimate ethical authority; and yet that very subjectivity, that sense of self, is said to be dissolving as well. Postmodern theorists have steadily eroded the traditional idea of the individual self, replacing it with the image of ourselves as simply the "intersections of competing discourses."[89] Believing that or not, the individual of today seems to have little confidence about his ability to make a difference, politically or psychologically. The hope that political action would gradually humanize industrial society seems in danger of giving way to what an observer saw as "a determination to survive the general wreckage or, more modestly, to hold one's life together in the face of mounting pressures."[85]

Some of those pressures undoubtedly come from having to deal with countless things our grandparents took for granted, if they thought of them at all, from the disintegration of the environment to the disintegration of social contracts and marriage vows. The breakdown of traditional forms of gender distinction and sexual preference has forced us to choose—from seemingly limitless options—how and who we love in particular and how we treat others in general. We live, lamented one critic, in a world where all the old comedically and dramatically interesting barriers to love's fulfillment have been dissolved, leaving us without even the material for good romantic movies.[125]

Dismantled as well are the boundaries between the stages of human life. It is said that first graders now run on schedules as rigid and focused as corporate CEOs, while CEOs go to camp to bond and climb mountains together: "Boomers go to fantasy baseball camps and chatter about what they'll do when they grow up. Men in their 50s turn back the clock with Propecia or Viagra, and senior citizens expect a life of vigor and engagement that defies conventional notions of old age."[6] While adults are struggling to get in touch with their inner child, children are committing monstrous crimes, and no one has any idea where the breakdown of barriers between childhood and adulthood will lead.

Overwhelmed by so much uncertainty, many have turned to the church. As Max Weber said, "If reality frightens you, the religion of your fathers is always there to welcome you back into its loving arms."[16] But today it is the dissolution of our familiar notion of reality itself that seems frightening, and even the religion of our fathers is being forced to grapple with the question of how the faithful should behave in a time of disintegrating values, when the definition of what constitutes sin seems to change along with society.

Elsewhere the threat of dissolving forms evokes a determination to hold firm at all costs. Every kind of fundamentalism, from Biblical to nationalistic to the authoritarian structure found in many supposedly New Age cults, thrives in times of anxiety. And today, an observer noted, "there are so many things to be anxious about, so many ways to be it."[73] The pervasive uncertainty, the postmodern insistence that our comfortable versions of reality are all just stories, has left some of us longing for absolutes. Fundamentalism is glad to oblige.

This summary of what's happening in the world is clearly subjective and far from complete, but the principle of disintegrating forms—and the resistance to that disintegration—does seem broadly characteristic of our time. The second question mentioned earlier: what, if anything, does it mean, or why do things seem to be falling apart, will be taken up in the following chapters, each of which considers this question of meaning from a particular point of view. The first two perspectives (chapters 3 and 4), which explore the effects of consumerism and environmental abuse, may be familiar to many of you, but read on. The next three points of view (chapters 5, 6, and 7) will undoubtedly be less familiar; cycles of time, qualities of time, and the evolution of human consciousness are not everyday concerns for most people. And yet, each of these three uncommon perspectives seems as effective as the earlier two in answering our questions about the meaning of the dissolution of form.

The last chapter looks at the same material and sees still another pattern, emphasizing again that reality is irreducibly complex and plural, unable to be exhausted by any single description, requiring instead a variety of points of view. This idea has been expressed repeatedly in the work of the artists and scientists who themselves will be observed from the different perspectives taken in these chapters. Picasso and Braque, Einstein, Marcel Duchamp, John Cage, and Andy Warhol were not only major influences in the development of twentieth-century Western culture. Each was also accomplished in the art of holding multiple perspectives.

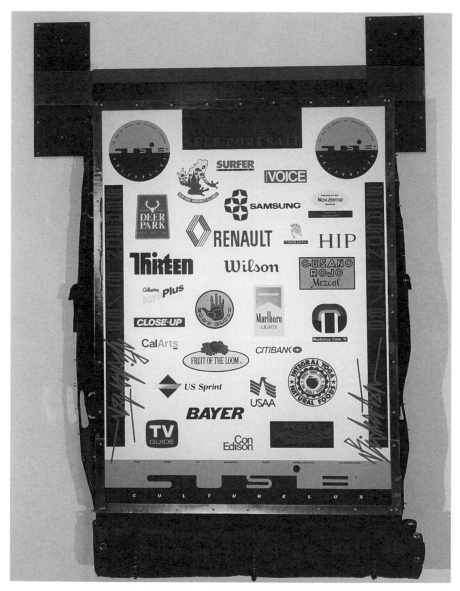

FIGURE 6. Ashley Bickerton, *Tormented Self-Portrait (Susie at Arles)*, 1987–1988. Synthetic polymer paint, bronze powder, and lacquer on wood, anodized aluminum, rubber, plastic, formica, leather, chrome-plated steel, and canvas, 89½ x 68¾ x 15¾ inches.

3

The World Is For Sale

What is the chief end of man? — to get rich.
In what way? — dishonestly if we can; honestly if we must.
Who is God, the only one and true? Money is God.
—Mark Twain

All that is solid melts into air.
—Karl Marx

"Capitalism has created the world as we know it."[167] The *New York Times'* Foreign Affairs editor said it plainly, and it is a very persuasive worldview. Economics has apparently replaced politics at the seat of power. The World Economic Forum, the Federal Reserve Board, and the Dow Jones are more closely watched than political summits. Corporations, not governments, appear to be in control of nations. If capitalism has indeed created the world as we know it, we must look to the marketplace for the source of twentieth-century trials. What might capitalism have to do with the dissolution of form and the collapse of time and space?

One could first observe that capitalist ideology lost its own form, became radically de-formed, over the course of the twentieth century. The early Puritan capitalists, guided by the Calvinist ethic, saved and reinvested the profit from their enterprises rather than spending it on their own comfort. Frugality and thrift were central to their lives. They worked hard to build up a business and then plowed the gains back into further development instead of indulging themselves in luxuries.[20] Things began to change around the beginning of the twentieth century with the spread of mass production and the desire of retailing giants to create an ever-increasing demand for their products. By the time Henry Ford adapted the process of a continual flow of parts on an assembly line to the making of the 1913 Model T, mass production and the mass marketing of standardized products were well under way.[143] A corresponding shift of focus to the numbers, to quantitative concerns, was not surprising. The more items that could be made, the bigger the profit.

And the possibilities for profit seemed limitless. The means of production were constantly being refined by technological improvements, which meant that more and more goods were continually being produced and needing to be consumed. By midcentury the virtues of mass consumption were unquestioned: economists blamed the 1930s depression on a lack of purchasing power, or underconsumption, and America's mass production industries were credited with winning World War II.[106] It began to seem inevitable that "conspicuous consumption," the indulgence in luxuries that was the enemy of early capitalist frugality, would turn into the new ideology. Capitalism had now become utterly dependent on the constant and increasing consumption of goods and services and was actively required, as Daniel Bell observed, "to endorse and foster a generally hedonistic, spendthrift, and throw-away ethic."[13]

FIGURE 7. Richard Hamilton, *Just What Is It That Makes Today's Homes So Different, So Appealing?* 1956. Collage.

By the 1950s it was clear that for the system to survive, not only must each individual constantly consume more goods and services (see figure 7 for Richard Hamilton's 1956 send-up of this trend), but new markets must be found for Western products. It has been said that the post-war spread of the consumer lifestyle around the world marks the most rapid and fundamental change in everyday existence the human species has ever experienced. In only a few generations, people all over the world became car drivers, mall shoppers, television watchers, and throwaway buyers.[35] The global market is even given credit for ending the Cold War. According to some observers, the Berlin Wall came down because of the failure of communist regimes in the East to provide consumer goods and services to the growing number of their young people who wanted to imitate Western lifestyles.[20]

With the disintegration of the Soviet Union and the freeing of Eastern Europe, countries around the globe unabashedly rushed to embrace capitalism and the American way — "from mutual funds to Madonna."[168] As the new forces of globalization swept the world, ancient civilizations struggled to become emerging markets, and the old world of international politics and national security began to seem utterly obsolete. The boundaries dissolved by capitalism were not only economic and political. In a world with more than 600 million television sets, viewers are as much consumers of ideas and values as they are of commercial products, and in many places the global economy collided head-on with the traditional values of ancient cultures. As a result some countries chose to adopt the trappings of capitalism without embracing the basic values — competition, efficiency, the legitimacy of profit — that make the system work. The Asian financial crisis of 1998 can be blamed in part on the fact that foreign investments ended up in the hands of borrowers whose traditional practices were very far from Western ideas of effective business conduct.[121]

To keep their economies growing in the future, Asian societies must at some point develop not only Western business practices but the Western consumer mentality as well, which means shifting from premodern thrift to the profligate habits of modern consumption. To the degree that Asians are successful in making this change, the whole region will look more and more like North America and Western Europe and less like traditional Asia. We are watching what one observer calls a "historical dissolution of place,"[65] and capitalism is apparently its source.

THE MEANING MAKERS

The dissolving of personal identity may also be attributed to the spread of capitalism. Through globalization, the individual of our time is continually reminded that different peoples have entirely different concepts of what the world is about — "all belief systems look around and become aware of all other belief systems"[4] — leading to the suspicion that what one calls reality is actually a social construction. Global capitalism further undermines traditional worldviews by promoting consumerism as today's guide to the good life. As a result, long-standing networks of social roles and the ideas of personal identity that go with them have begun to disappear.

The sprawling cities of the Third World are filled with people who, attracted by capitalism's promise of a better life, have freed themselves from the confines of local villages and the bonds of clan and tribe. But as Peter Berger points out, a high price is paid for this freedom: "The individual comes to experience himself as being *alone* in a way that is unthinkable in traditional society—deprived of the firm solidarity of his collectivity, uncertain of the norms by which his life is to be governed, finally uncertain of who or what he is."[15] His experience, in other words, mirrors the experience of the Western individual of today, "liberated" through the breakdown of distinctions of class, sex, religion, and other social forms that once gave meaning to an individual's experience of his place in time. Will our Third World hero ultimately find, like his Western counterpart, that consuming has become the main social, economic, and cultural process in his life? Probably. The ideology of consumerism, that the meaning of life is to be found in buying packaged things and experiences,[20] is the leading replacement for traditional values around the world (figure 8).

It was once thought that when people were freed from economic need they would try to realize their potential as individual human beings and strive for self-actualization. It now seems clear that in the United States at least, people simply keep consuming more and more. The exporting world may rejoice, as we will see later, but one economist sees our passion for expensive goods as a debilitating disease, a disease that wastes trillions of dollars a year and to one extent or another has each of us in its grip.[27] Others point out that consuming has no limits today because it can never fill the need it is now responding to: the need for meaning in one's life.

With the disintegration of other definers of status and group membership, what you buy tends to become who you are. Ashley Bickerton's *Tormented Self-Portrait* (see figure 6) displays an assortment of corporate logos and labels of

FIGURE 8. Barbara Kruger, *Untitled* (I shop therefore I am), 1987. Photographic silkscreen on vinyl, 111 x 113 inches.

products—Bayer aspirin, *Surfer* magazine, *Village Voice*, Citibank, Integral Yoga Natural Foods, Marlboro cigarettes—that the artist has consumed or used, satirizing himself as the sum of his chosen brand names and institutions. In the words of one cultural historian, "consumption is now absolutely inseparable from identity ... our purchases are creations of *meaning.*"5

When we are what we buy, our lives, including our inner lives, tend to be organized around economic principles. By equating everything with its market value, we end up "seeking answers to questions about what is worthwhile, honorable, and even what is real, in the marketplace."89 It is therefore not surprising to find advertising, television, and media in general so intensely permeating our lives. In a society of consumers, who is better suited to form our "representations," the pictures and stories of how life is to be lived? No longer the artists or the priests, but the salesmen of the world are now charged with creating the significance of our lives. Advertising has become what one social critic called "the dominant meaning-making system of modern life."158

The primary medium for these instructional representations is of course TV, whose programs are described as the scheduled interruptions between marketing bulletins. Here too distinctions are breaking down; products are increasingly diffused throughout the program segment, and it is sometimes not clear when the narrative segment ends and the commercial begins. When TV ads turn out to be more creative and ingenious than the program itself (not at all a rare event), the lines between art and commerce are further dissolved.

Advertising today is described as the most pervasive form of propaganda in history, the device through which the virtues of consuming are elaborated and its images transmitted around the world. As the generator of worldwide consumer culture, advertising is accused of collapsing disparate peoples into a monolithic global style built around jeans and Nikes,

Cokes and Big Macs. "From high culture to folk, from high brow to low, from Aesthetica to Vulgaria, commercial speech is not so much shouting down competing voices as enlisting them to sing the same tune."[158] Most transnational advertisers have no reservations about reshaping the values of whole societies in order to create a "homogenized culture of indulgence" that stimulates consumption of their products and services while advancing corporate political interests.[75]

CONSUMER CHOICE & LIBERATION MARKETING

In this country one of capitalism's great successes has been the dissolving of distinctions between individual freedom and consumer choice. Social critics in the 1950s, alarmed by the spread of mass culture in the United States, began to predict a flattening sameness, but as it turned out the domestic market thrives not on uniformity but on the appearance of variety.[18] The television generation recognizes the illusory nature of consumer choice. They know that there is no real distinction to be made between networks or between all shows within a particular genre. But as one observer points out, the absorbing of superfluous choice is what we do best:

M&Ms come in 70 different packages. Revlon makes 158 shades of lipstick. Crest toothpaste comes in 36 sizes and shapes and flavors. Sony produces more than 100 varieties of Walkman devices, Seiko makes more than 3,000 watches, and Philips has 800 models of color TVs. Don't even think about sneakers.[158]

Even fundamentalists who have elected to give up all other freedoms of choice retain access to consumer choice. And the more strictly these groups try to differentiate themselves from whatever might today be called the mainstream, the more profitable for a constantly diversifying market.

The ability of consumer capitalism to absorb and exploit diversity is matched by its successes in dissolving opposition, diluting protest by incorporating those images into capitalism's own program. Perhaps its greatest achievement has been the assimilation of the original counterculture of the 1960s. According to one version of the sixties uprising, Western "metanarratives" (the usually heroic stories that justify our history) became increasingly suspect with the advent of the Civil Rights and feminist movements, the rewriting of Native American history, and the discovery of the role industrialism has played in degrading the environment.[89] The intense questioning of received doctrines then combined with the cynicism generated by Vietnam and Watergate to fuel new social movements and anticapitalist fervor.

But by the late seventies the rebellion of the sixties had already been made marketable, defused by the absorptive power of consumer capitalism and the wit of its salesmen. It turned out that the market was fully capable of "incorporating into itself rebellion as a lifestyle, black consciousness as a pop-culture and a consumer fashion, and hipsterism as a joking irony that ridiculed the act of selling even as it sold everything to everybody."[33] Rock music's metamorphosis from an almost moral force in the sixties into an unbeatable money-making machine in the eighties has been well documented.[50] The idealistic fledgling computer industry suffered (or enjoyed) the same fate. Many of the earliest person-to-person computer networks were deeply rooted in the sixties counterculture, and in fact, Stewart Brand, the founder of WELL (Whole Earth 'Lectronic Link), claims that the personal computer revolutionaries *were* the counterculture. Personal computers and the PC industry were actually created by young iconoclasts who had seen both the LSD revolution and the political revolution fail. "Computers for the people!" became the latest rallying cry in the same campaign.[117]

But the personal computer revolution also failed, in the sense that what was once fantasized as being the largest functioning anarchy in the world was largely absorbed into corporate service. The focus of the technology world is now centered on strategies for winning big-business clients, not individual users, and innovation is accommodated to huge accounts like Exxon and General Motors. "These guys are the business," claims an observer. "They drive the networks. They drive the innovation. What they do, you follow."[126]

In the visual arts, the dissolving of distinctions between high culture and so-called mass or popular culture may also have begun as a political ideal — Andy Warhol's images of Campbell's soup cans and Coke bottles have been interpreted by many critics as political statements aimed at the commodity fetishism of the times[65] — but these ended up deep in the commercial black as well. And if the dissolving of boundaries between high art and low was not originally a marketing tool, as others believe it was, it apparently did contribute to the practice of assessing works of art by a monetary standard alone. Today, we are told by a cultural historian, "artists, gallery owners, critics, and public wallow

FIGURE 9. Andy Warhol, *One Dollar Bill*, 1962, synthetic polymer paint and silkscreen on canvas, 52 x 72 inches.

together in the 'anything goes.'"[90] And the reality of the "anything goes," he adds, is that of money (figure 9.)

Where once we had movements for change, we now have products. As Thomas Frank writes in *Conglomerates and the Media,* advertising knows that business has conquered the world, and it offers you in defense

not just soaps that get your whites whiter, but soaps that lib-
erate you, soda pops that are emblems of individualism, ra-
dios of resistance, carnivalesque cars, and counterhegemonic
hamburgers. ... Liberation marketing imagines consumers
breaking free from the old order, tearing loose from the

shackles with which capitalism has bound us, escaping the routine of bureaucracy and hierarchy.

What Frank calls liberation marketing takes fully into account the old mass-culture critique that consumerism is conformity, acknowledges it, and dissolves it—with products that "set you free."[44]

Capitalism may also be held accountable for the collapse of our familiar perceptions of time and space, for speeding up the pace of life and overcoming the barriers of distance. Multinational corporations have increasingly become the controllers of the telecommunication networks that allow businesses to operate around the clock. Currency traders in all parts of the world now see the same information at the same time and act on it simultaneously. From Hong Kong to Toronto, trading in Sony and General Motors stock goes on twenty-four hours a day, creating a single market, independent of time and space—and incredibly volatile. The world has already felt the impact of the frenzy of investment, trade, and technological change that can build up a nation's economy overnight and just as quickly bring it down.

An increasingly rapid rhythm of styling and fashion changes in cars, clothes, and cosmetics assures a quickening of obsolescence as well. The exemplar of modern marketing is the women's fashion industry, where almost all clothing, regardless of quality, goes out of style and is replaced long before it is worn out. The former chairman of a major department store explains: "Basic utility cannot be the foundation of a prosperous apparel industry. ... We must accelerate obsolescence."[85] The manufacturers of computers and cell phones, skateboards and software, respond to the same imperative. For centuries generations of people succeeded one another surrounded by objects that had longer lives than they, but who today finds it odd that many generations of *objects* now follow upon one another at an ever-accelerating pace during a single human lifetime?[10]

Critics of consumer capitalism point out that its dependence on rapid change has led to the disappearance of a sense of history in our culture, to a pervasive depthlessness, a "perpetual present" from which all memory of tradition has disappeared.[18] Writing for *Harvard Design Magazine,* Ellen Dunham-Jones sees capitalism's compressing of time as central to cultural anxiety and disintegration: "The social contracts that supported our grandparents have been ruptured. Marriage vows, the homestead, corporate stability, and job security—all have suffered in the ever-evolving, nonstop world of GATT and NAFTA, of cyberspace, freeways, 24-hour convenience marts, and other manifestations of post-industrialism."[35]

DISSOLVING THE ENVIRONMENT

Every country in the world is experiencing environmental deterioriation, but none so dramatically as those that have made rapid economic growth their primary national goal. As Kenneth Gergen points out, wherever upward scrambling has become the meaning of life, the planet is being laid waste:

> It is now hardly newsworthy that petroleum reserves are being depleted, lakes and rivers are polluted or drying up, the ozone layer is growing thin, forests are disappearing, underground water supplies are becoming undrinkable, air unbreathable, beaches unswimmable, noise levels unendurable, fish and animal species extinct, and so on. Pity the primitive with only a handful of concerns; in the service of progress we moderns can now produce them by the hundreds.[46]

The main concern of a great many contemporary "primitives," of course, is how to be more like us. On local television sets or movie screens in villages around the world, the land of milk and honey—the West—is nightly on display.[35] On the Bolivian antiplano, Quechua-speaking Indian communities use portable satellite dishes to tune in *Miami Vice;* Australian aborigines in the outback are said to be particularly fond of *Seinfeld.* The American entertainment industry (motion pictures, music, and videos as well as television programming) is our nation's second biggest exporter, and it is the lifestyle-setter for a developing world that is longing to live, if not the life of *Dynasty,* at least that of Jerry, George, and Elaine. The loser in this electronic seduction is inevitably the environment. "Because the 170 million people in Indonesia have the same aspirations as anyone in the United States," announced the Indonesian government, "20 percent of our forests must be converted to plantations to produce teak, rubber, rice, coffee, and other agricultural crops."[72]

It is easy for outsiders to warn against the long-term environmental deterioration that is brought on by destroying woodlands or damming rivers in underdeveloped countries, but such an attitude is said to be "akin to a glutton admonishing a beggar on the evil of carbohydrates—he lacks a certain moral authority."[60] Environmental concerns must seem utterly inconsequential to people who are desperately trying to escape living conditions that we in the United States would never tolerate. Once human beings experience electricity, running water, and telephones, they want more of them, no matter what the cost to the environment. Would we—do we—behave differently? According to one calculation, the average American baby represents thirty-five times the future environmental damage of an Indian child. The United States consistently heads the list of countries with the highest greenhouse gas emissions, including twice the CFCs (chlorofluorocarbons), of its nearest competitor.[72] And after a brief period of conservation, we are again using energy as if it were limitless.

All the indulgences of humankind, not only the worldwide increase of emissions but the destruction of tropical forests, the draining of wetlands and aquifers, and the overgrazing of plains and savannahs are seen as contributing causes of a possible "greenhouse effect" that could change natural ecologies in irremediable ways. Each new suggestion of global warming heightens the sense that we are all in the same boat, and that the boat is disintegrating. As the climate changes and sea levels rise, even the most environmentally responsible societies will be affected. This is certainly not news, but Western levels of consuming continue to climb. More than five trillion dollars' worth of goods and services are consumed each year in this country, and it is now easier than ever to finance extra spending. So ardent is our consumption that we appear to be able indefinitely to sustain faltering economies around the world. Overseas we are referred to as the industrial world's "consumers of last resort" and urged, in the interest of global prosperity, to keep shopping.[27] At home we are warned that we must consume to keep ourselves employed: "If no one buys, no one sells, and if no one sells, no one works."[35] We are, it seems, on an irreversible track leading to the wholesale destruction of the environment.

Those who argue that lowering our rate of consuming on purpose, individually and collectively, would precipitate economic disaster both at home and abroad ignore the probable alternative: continuing to deform and degrade the earth guarantees an even greater level of misfortune. According to one observer, if we attempt to preserve the consumer economy indefinitely, "ecological forces will dismantle it savagely. If we proceed to dismantle it gradually ourselves, we will have the opportunity of replacing it with a low-consumption economy that can endure."[35] Either way, our familiar economic form, the rampant consumer capitalism that seems to have caused the breakdown of so much of the world's cultural and environmental order, will itself be dissolved.

FIGURE 10. Georges Braque, *Castle at La Roche-Guyon*, 1909.

4

The World Is Alive & Unwell

*The one space reaches through all Beings,
World inner space. The birds fly silently
through us. Oh, I who wants to grow,
I look outside, and in me grows the tree.*
—Rainer Maria Rilke, *"Es winkt zu Fühlung"*
("Everything beckons to us to perceive it ")

*All the errors and follies of magic, religion, and mystical tradition
are outweighed by the one great wisdom they contain—
the awareness of humanity's organic embeddedness
in a complex and natural system.*
—Philip Slater, *Earthwalk*

In developing countries, public health seems largely to have been sacrificed to the drive for economic growth. None of the world's twenty most populous cities can claim to meet the World Health Organization's clear-air standards; in Mexico City seven out of ten newborn babies have excessively high levels of lead in their blood.[72] Countries with high income levels appear to be experiencing increases in the incidence of cancer, respiratory illnesses, stress disorders, birth defects, and falling sperm counts. A growing body of evidence seems to link all these phenomena to the by-products of economic growth: air and water pollution, chemical additives and pesticide residues in food, high noise levels, and perhaps increased exposure to electromagnetic radiation.[75] But as physically unhealthy as the environment seems to have become for the earth's residents, the effect of its deterioration on the human mind may be worse. From the perspective taken in this chapter, the breakdown of nature's form is affecting our psychological integrity—and thus contributing to the dissolution of cultural form.

THE CONNECTEDNESS OF THINGS

In antiquity, and still today among traditional peoples, it is generally believed that human beings and the world around them are intimately connected and mutually sustaining within an invisible, but nevertheless real, network of forces. Western science, in contrast, has tended to see the world as composed of separate and independent entities, each holding its own place in space and time. The Western view was shaken early in the twentieth century, however, when physicists fused time and space, translated matter into energy, and found formerly empty space to be filled with invisible "fields." Dynamic process became physics' new law of nature, and nothing thereafter could safely be thought of as being isolated from anything else—even, or especially, the human being and his environment. At the very least, notes an observer, "we are forced to conclude that the 'world' is not independent of us. ... Everything, it seems, is related to everything else."[16]

A similar perspective emerged in early-twentieth-century art. At almost the same moment that Einstein was demonstrating the interchangeability of energy and matter, two painters in Paris were beginning to devise ways of making objects and space interpenetrate so as to be almost indistinguishable from one another. Georges Braque and Pablo Picasso were creating a system by which they could reveal the interlocking of phenomena, depicting processes instead of static states of being, confounding architecture and natural landscape (figure 10) in what is described as "a shimmering fabric of dismembered planes."[119] Their way of painting became known as Cubism.

"To edge their way in behind appearances"[159] was the goal of the Cubists. They acknowledged the influence of Paul Cézanne, of whom one observer remarked, "He painted things as he painted human beings, because he was endowed with the gift of divining the inner life in everything."[69] According to another, Cézanne made looking the equivalent of touching: "He made an art stripped of everything except the unseen made corporeal and solid. He went to nature like someone going to Mass."[25] Shortly before his death in 1906, Cézanne painted a series of landscapes of Mont Sainte-Victoire (figure 11), in which he fragmented and simplified whole planes, reducing them to transparent cubes that reveal the inner structure of mountain, trees, and houses.[78]

Inspired by Cézanne, the Cubists worked to see things not only from above or in profile but also from within, experiencing the relationship between forms and the space around them as a dynamic, continuously changing process. In this first great phase of modern art, Braque and Picasso gave to space the same colors, textures, and substantiality that they gave to material objects. By reducing the form of their objects to combinations of cubes, cylinders, facets, and

FIGURE 11. Paul Cézanne, *Mont Sainte-Victoire*, 1904–1906.

planes, they were able to paint the interactions between them as well. Braque had worked earlier in the style of the Fauves (wild beasts, so-called because of their seemingly violent use of color), a style characterized by an "all-overness" and "everywhere-dense continuum of events."[15] He wanted to see the object as something woven into a network of spatial relations with everything else that surrounded it, a continuum of interdependent activity.

The immediate influence of Cubism on other artists is perhaps most dramatically demonstrated in two paintings of

trees by the Dutch painter Piet Mondrian. In the earlier
painting (figure 12), Mondrian's sense of an underlying di-
vinity in nature is expressed in the melding of trunk,
branches, earth, and sky into a living whole, not unlike
landscapes painted earlier by his countryman Van Gogh.
"Just as the trembling, skeletal branches are woven directly
into the fabric of the sky ... so, too, do the tree's roots blend
imperceptibly with the earth that nourishes them."[119] Three
years later, after an encounter with Cubism, which he believed provided him with a means of unveiling the spiritual

FIGURE 12. Piet Mondrian, *The Red Tree*, 1908–1909.

FIGURE 13. *Composition No. 3* (Trees), Piet Mondrian, 1912.

geometry of the world, Mondrian painted the composition of trees in figure 13. A third painting from the early 1920s (figure 14) shows the further evolution of his distinctive style. In Mondrian's eyes, the Cubists' penetration of external form and their equal treatment of matter and so-called empty space were vehicles with which to articulate the ordered continuum that lay behind the surfaces of reality.

IMPLICATE ORDERS

Though Cubism itself fell to the first world war, scientists have continued to find indications of a continuum. Although most physicists are still treating "fields" as more or less discrete phenomena, the eminent theorist David Bohm speaks of the "unbroken wholeness of the totality of existence as an undivided flowing movement without borders." Ultimately, Bohm believes, the entire universe—including human beings, their laboratories, and observing instruments—must be understood as a single undivided whole, in which analysis into separate and independently existing parts would have no fundamental status: "What is implied by this proposal is that what we call empty space contains an immense background of energy, and that matter as we know it is a small, 'quantized' wavelike excitation on top of this background, rather like a tiny ripple on a vast sea."[21]

Bohm sees space as an ocean of energy, full rather than empty, analogous to the plenum theorized by Zeno and the School of Parmenides in ancient Greece. The earliest opposition to the idea of a plenum came from Democritus in the fourth century BC, who proposed instead a world view that for the first time conceived of space as empty, a void in which material particles or atoms move around. This atomistic view enjoyed a long reign of influence on Western science, with residues lasting to the present day. We are, as one

The World Is Alive & Unwell · 47

observer noted, still locked into a "parts mentality,"[163] trying to explain how separate things join together even as we construct various field theories.

What Bohm is suggesting is that at a level we can't perceive—the level of unbroken wholeness—there is an "implicate order" out of which everything, all seemingly separate entities, arises. This idea of an underlying order connecting apparently unrelated events has found support in several scientific contexts, not the least of which is John Bell's work with nonlocality. It was Bell who first showed that two electrons or two photons that have been separated from one another will remain actively correlated in a way that is direct, instantaneous, and not the result of some intermediary force or field. One explanation for this kind of nonlocal connection would be that quantum forms actually unfold out of a deeper implicate order, in which case two electrons that are separated in space would still be in contact at the implicate level.[112] Bell's demonstration was again confirmed recently in studies conducted at the University of Geneva, where physicists involved in particle experimentation established more firmly than ever that two photons separated across great distances remain "correlated ... in some funny mathematical way that defies common sense."[68]

Bohm's idea of an implicate order is of particular interest to scientists working with chaos and complexity theory, in which chaos is defined not as an absence or lack of order but as an infinitely complex order, an "underlying interconnectedness that exists in apparently random events."[23] Similar ideas are gaining ground in the biological sciences, stimulated by Rupert Sheldrake's proposal of the existence of invisible fields acting across time and space to maintain species

FIGURE 14. Piet Mondrian, *Composition with Red, Yellow, Blue and Black*, 1921.

uniformity and evolution. According to this British biologist, "the idea that everything is determined in advance and in principle predictable has given way to the ideas of indeterminism, spontaneity, and chaos. The invisible organizing powers of animate nature are once again emerging in the form of fields."[131] Sheldrake's theory of morphic resonance holds that patterns of behavior can change throughout an entire species, not because each individual has taken the time to learn the new behavior but because the content of their morphogenetic field has changed. What affects one, in theory, affects them all.

In what he calls "an updated version of premechanistic animism," Sheldrake looks on all nature as alive. From this point of view, even molecules are organisms rather than inert atoms of matter and contain patterns of energetic activity within fields. Sheldrake's theories are independently supported by the findings of several physicists, among them Evan Harris Walker, who mathematically explored the animism implicit in quantum mechanics and concluded that every particle in the universe possesses consciousness,[16] and Freeman Dyson, for whom "mind is already inherent in every electron."[31]

Adding to the credibility of these views is the work of Gregory Bateson, a brilliant scientist whose worldview included the perspectives of cybernetics, information and systems theory, anthropology, and psychology. Bateson concluded that it is not only legitimate but logically inevitable to assume the existence of mental processes—what he called Mind—on all levels of natural phenomena of sufficient complexity: cells, organs, tissues, organisms, animal and human groups, ecosystems, and even the earth and the universe as a whole.[9] He saw that Western man, in treating the world around him as expendable resources, was beginning to threaten his own survival. For Bateson the true unit of survival, and of Mind, was not organism or species, but organism *plus* environment, species *plus* environment. In the words of one of his students: "If you choose the wrong unit, and believe it is somehow all right to pollute Lake Erie until it loses its Mind, then you will go a little insane yourself, because you are a sub-Mind in a larger Mind that you have driven a bit crazy."[16]

The nature of the connection between organisms and their environment was a question that also intrigued the British atmospheric scientist James Lovelock, whose Gaia hypothesis views the earth itself as a biological organism, capable of regulating the conditions necessary for all terrestrial life. In his remarkable book *Gaia: A New Look at Life on Earth*, Lovelock found evidence of complex feedback mechanisms that may actually be maintaining not only the stability of the earth's temperature but also the concentration of key components—salt, oxygen, ammonia, and ozone—in the atmosphere, oceans, and soil.[88] As observed by his colleague Lynn Margulis:

> The steadiness of mean planetary temperature for the past three thousand million years, the 700-million-year maintenance of Earth's reactive atmosphere between high-oxygen levels of combustibility and low-oxygen levels of asphyxiation, and the apparently continuous removal of hazardous salts from the oceans—all these point to mammal-like purposefulness in the organization of life as a whole.[94]

THE WORLD SOUL

Though Lovelock and Margulis were the first to present scientific evidence for the idea of the earth as an organism or living system, similar perspectives have appeared in other times and places, going back at least as far as Plato's description of the *anima mundi,* the soul of the world. In the *Timaeus*(36), Plato describes the world as a living being with intelligence in soul and soul "woven right through from the center to the outermost heaven." Contemporary philosophers have taken a fresh look at the idea that qualities of soul are not limited to human beings or perhaps even animals or plants, but in some sense belong to the essential activity of the earth. According to Robert Sardello, if we perceive things merely as objects, we miss the soul quality of all that surrounds us—and fail to recognize the connection between our own psychic life and the soul of the world.[124]

In his books on the life of the soul, Sardello explores indications from Eastern traditions that the individual and the earth are inseparably bound to one another through a common membrane, known in esoteric literature as the subtle, or "etheric," body (the pranamayakosa of yoga and Tibetan Buddhism). It is this individual subtle body, the point of focus in Chinese acupuncture and tai ch'i, that continues to suffer in phantom limb pain; its momentary withdrawal from the physical foot gives the sensation that the foot has gone to sleep. Called the "life body" in other traditions, these subtle energy fields control the vitality—the animating principle—of the physical being. Sardello believes that because each individual subtle body is interwoven with that of the earth, our personal health and the health of the world coincide. It follows that "as we neglect and abuse the things of the world, we are at the same time abusing ourselves."[101]

If these observations are correct, if we are indeed linked to the earth in some profoundly intimate way, what might human beings be feeling on a soul or psychic level in a deteriorating environment? Today an estimated 330 million people worldwide are suffering from depression, or what one researcher calls "malignant sadness." According to the head of epidemiology at the World Health Organization, unipolar major depression will be the world's second most debilitating illness by 2020, surpassed only by cardiovascular disease.[36] Sardello feels that the prevalence of grief in our time is something more than a personal psychological process belonging to individuals. For him, the grieving we see all around us is actually the human experience of the suffering of the earth. Those who grieve deeply in these times are expressing what we all feel and are afraid to face—the dying of the earth: "As long as this is denied, what belongs to the world will continue to be interpreted as only personal psychological suffering, when in fact it is at the same time a world suffering."[124]

These contemporary observers do not agree in all particulars. Sardello sees radiation devices to be as threatening as visible air pollution; Lovelock believes primitive farming methods in the tropics are as degrading to the environment as industrialism. But the point that they and others are making is that the world is alive and the damage we have done to her is making us sad and crazed. From the perspective taken here, this loss of psychological well-being leads in turn to the dissolution of cultural forms.

And again the possibilities of a reversal seem slim. Correcting the human misuse of natural resources is complicated not only by politics, economics, and personal greed but also by the addition each decade of a billion people to the family of man. The number of individuals on the planet rose from four billion in 1975 to six billion in 1999. Projected figures for 2025 approach eight or nine billion, with 95 percent of future population growth estimated to occur in developing countries,[72] countries that largely aspire to a Western standard of living. "For every convert to environmentalism in the West, there are probably at least two or three new consumers being produced and socialized somewhere in the world—perhaps many more."[20] At this point the most significant threats to the environment are not only the excessive demands and wasteful habits of affluent countries but the billions of new consumers being born into the developing world. To seek solutions in the decreasing fertility rate of industrialized nations, or in the slowing of population growth in places like Africa with a high death rate from disease, drought, or famine is nonsensical. It is said that the global environment cannot sustain even two billion people living like American consumers, much less six or eight billion.[35]

According to Lovelock, if we continue to encroach on Gaia's functional power in ways that ultimately disable her, we might find ourselves one day in the lifelong permanent job of planetary maintenance engineer. He maintains that the capacity of the earth to regulate conditions for terrestrial life depends on "core" regions, those that lie between latitudes 45 degrees north and 45 degrees south, which includes the tropical forests and scrub lands. Devastation of these tropical ecosystems could eventually diminish the earth's ability to modify the consequences of our disruptive behavior throughout the planet. If that were to happen, "Gaia would have retreated into the muds, and the ceaseless intricate task of keeping all of the global cycles in balance would be ours."[88]

Compared with other predictions, some of which will be explored from the perspective taken in the next chapter, Lovelock's vision of planetary maintenance may be considered optimistic. But even the darker prospects seem in the long run somehow just. It is perhaps only natural, after all, that humanity would reach, and then extend beyond, its limits to growth. As Duane Elgin observes, the fact that almost every organism seeks to exploit its ecological niche to the fullest extent means that the tendency to overshoot and collapse is a common occurrence in natural systems. As this is the first time humanity has had the power to regard the entire planet as our "ecological niche," we have no experience in exercising restraint as a species:

> We learn through experience, and we have never encountered this situation before; so we should not be surprised if a great tragedy is necessary to awaken the evolutionary intelligence of humanity.[38]

FIGURE 15. Robert Delaunay, *Champ-de-Mars: The Red Tower* (Eiffel Tower), 1911–1923.

5

The World Is Ending

The smoky candle end of time
Declines.
— T.S. Eliot, *Burbank*, 1920

... according to the Maya, the end of the present world
will come about on 24 December 2011.
— Colin Renfrew and Paul Bahn,
Archaeology, 1991

Whether or not one sees the earth as a living organism in trouble, a great many people do seem to be experiencing a sense of approaching crisis, a feeling that we have reached a turning point of some kind. There are many scenarios that seem to validate, if not create, this unease. For example, the environmental deterioration described in the last chapter suggests to many observers a dismal future:

Within a generation the world will become a superheated pressure cooker in which the human family is crushed by the combined and unrelenting forces of an expanding world population, a dramatically destabilized global climate, dwindling supplies of nonrenewable energy, and mounting environmental pollution.[38]

Other ingredients for disaster, any or all of which can be combined with those just quoted, include nuclear accidents or wars, cyberterrorism, economic collapse, plague from known, unknown, or newly resistant diseases, and social disintegration.

What happens, for example, if social turbulence increases at the same rate as the world's population? In places like Afghanistan, the Middle East, the Horn of Africa, the rimlands of the former USSR, Central America, and elsewhere, there are fast-growing, youthful populations with frustrated economic and social expectations. Not only nationalistic fervor but various kinds of environmental collapse could lead to greater instability and conflict in these underdeveloped regions: roving gangs of marauders, fights over water and food, abuse of minority groups, even open warfare between countries.[73] The number of refugees worldwide is already on the rise, and according to one observer: "There may soon be an even larger flood of environmental refugees as societies break down or experience civil war in the face of natural catastrophes."[72]

If millenarian sentiments remain strong, religious disputes could intensify, and terrorists may attempt to time their acts of violence to coincide with what some think will be the Apocalypse, described in the last book of the Bible as the end of the age of history. In the last decades of the twentieth century, millennial themes in the West shifted from nuclear war to images of environmental catastrophe and back again to war in the Balkans or the Middle East. Apocalyptic prophecies have also been stimulated by what some see as the "sheer internal decay and indulgence" of Western society and by the process of computerization, with some millenarians suggesting that the Antichrist will turn out to be a computer.[141]

Others see the current situation not as a prelude to apocalypse but as an accurate reflection of our historical placement near the end of a cycle of time. For William Strauss and Neil Howe, cultural historians based in Washington, DC, modern history does not move to a rhythm created by the institutions or even the economies of world powers, but to the rhythm of life itself. They believe that we are approaching the final phase of a historical cycle that renews itself every eighty years or so — about the length of a human life — and is composed of four phases, each lasting some twenty years and roughly corresponding to what we call a generation. Although the concept of the generation as a historical agent for change goes back at least far as ancient Greece, Strauss and Howe find that in no previous setting has the cycle of generations "propelled this wheel of time with more force than in America."[144] From their point of view, a generalized disintegration of form would be well suited to the phase we presently occupy in their approximately eighty-year cycle, a phase named by the authors the Unraveling.

The four phases (or "turnings") within their cycle are described as follows. The High — the first turning — is a period of confident expansion and strengthening of civic life as a new order replaces the old. In the second turning, the Awakening, the outer world begins to feel insignificant in comparison to the inner world, and spiritual exploration and rebellion against the now-established new order are just pursuits. The third phase, the Unraveling, is an increasingly troubled time in which public trust wanes in the midst of a fragmenting culture, disagreements over values, and cynical alienation; decisive public action becomes difficult with the authority of all government at a low point. Finally, we experience a "Crisis"—the fourth turning—which represents a major discontinuity, ultimately leading to the replacement of the old order by a completely new one that will be celebrated in the following High.

The authors find evidence of this cycle dating back to the American Revolution, but it can be most clearly observed within our own lifetime. After the last Crisis, defined by the depression and war years of 1929 to 1945, the cycle began again. The designated first turning, the High, opened with the end of World War II and ended with the Kennedy assassination in 1963:

> By June 1946, the nation realized that the postwar mood shift was permanent and massive. ... Large institutions were regarded as effective, government as powerful, science as benign, schools as good, careers as reliable, families as strong, and crime as under control. Government could afford to do almost anything it wanted, while still balancing its budget. ... Worker productivity and family incomes grew at the fastest pace ever measured, with no end in sight.[144]

The threat to group survival represented by the recent crisis stimulated the desire for investment, growth, and strength, which in turn produced an era of prosperity and political stability. Gender distinctions reached their widest point, and life in general tended toward the conventional.

The assassination of John F. Kennedy in 1963 marked the end of the High and our entry into the roughly twenty-year phase of the Awakening, a period generally characterized by the exalting of rights over duties, ideals over institutions, self over society, and creativity over conformism. In what some have called the Consciousness Revolution, self-expression took precedence over self-control. "Wealthy kids dressed down, donned unisex styles, and became self-declared 'freaks' as if to reject the affluence and civic order of their elders."[144] Forty-four percent of college students in 1970 believed that violence was justified to bring about change, displaying the clenched fist as their emblem. T-shirts and jeans were the uniform, corporate greed the enemy. A New Age was celebrated with claims of a "sovereign right of self-discovery," which was to be realized through a human potential movement that was seen as a reaction to mechanized, industrialized thinking.

Strauss and Howe date the beginning of the third turning—the Unraveling—at around 1984 and its ending at approximately 2004. "From TV talk shows to dependency groups to church basements, the search for personal meaning started with the direct experience of the individual." These self-discovered meanings were then validated by others attracted to the individual's own niche group (which might be based on sex, race, religion, occupation, even gun ownership). As niche groups strengthened, they began erasing the idea of a universal worldview in favor of local and immediate perspectives. Unlike in the High, there was no such thing now as "normal" public opinion. By the early

1990s, America's niche group conflict was identified with the so-called Culture Wars, and the characteristics of the Unraveling were becoming increasingly distinct: weakening government, social fragmentation, and relentless individualism—"a nation becoming ever more diverse and decentralized, its citizens inhabiting a high-tech world of tightening global ties and loosening personal ones, its Web sites multiplying and its culture splintering."[144]

The fourth turning, the Crisis (c. 2005–2025), is expected to be a time of radical change reminiscent of the disaster scenarios mentioned earlier, stimulated by either fiscal crises, acts of terrorism, new communicable viruses, civic decay, debt, global disorder, or some combination of these. This last quadrant of the cycle is described as an era of trial and suffering when "great worldly perils boil off the clutter and complexity of life." We are assured, however, that the Crisis is not necessarily a time of unrelieved tragedy: "Though it can produce destruction, it can also produce uncommon vision, heroism, and a sudden elevation of the human condition."[144] And it does lead again to the next High.

The cycle defined by Strauss and Howe is the latest of a great many efforts throughout history to find meaningful patterns in time. Among those known to us, there appear to be three dominant ways of picturing time's flow. The one most familiar to the Western mentality portrays time as linear, moving forward in a direction that in religious contexts may imply a final goal. By contrast, for the ancient and classical worlds—and still today for some Asian cultures—historical time is cyclical, always returning at regular intervals to the same point, usually after declining from the purity of its beginning. The third category sees time's course as a combination of the first two, obeying an underlying cyclical law while simultaneously moving forward. The movement of time in this pattern is often pictured as rhythms, waves, or spirals.[26]

What Strauss and Howe have given us is essentially a small-scale version of cyclic historical decline, the second of those above, which is best known from the Greek sequence of declining ages (from Gold to Silver to Bronze to Iron) and the yugas (Krita, Treta, Dvapara, and Kali) of the Hindu Manvantara. Theirs is an appropriate updating of this concept at a time when many observers feel that society is indeed unraveling. One finds extensions of this perspective scattered through the daily newspaper: a media critic describes as rough and unforgiving the business of tracking "the collapse of global civilization week in and week out as television shimmies the limbo bar of popular culture just a little lower for us all";[91] in an unrelated article in the same issue, reference is made to "these cynical, weaselly, sordid, frightening times."[100] Elsewhere cultural historians suggest that "society has reached the bottom of a historical cycle from which things can only improve even if, first of all, they have to get a little worse."[26]

Twentieth-century poets have also placed us at the dissolute end of a historical cycle. Both Yeats and Eliot wrote extensively on the collapse of a Western civilization that had originated with the birth of Christ. In *The Second Coming* ("Things fall apart: the center cannot hold ..."), W.B. Yeats, who was hospitable to astrological ideas, used the changes of the moon to relate the phases of 2,000 years of European history from the birth of Christ to his own wayward century. At around the same time (c. 1920), T.S. Eliot was portraying the history of Western civilization as the movement from youth to senility, a process of aging that results in a corruption of faith and will in those of us living in the final phase.[138] In Eliot's *Gerontion,* the aged narrator embodies the decay of society; he has no character apart from the dissolute habits of Christian civilization in its senescence. The poet expanded this vision in *The Waste Land,* a poetic exploration of a fallen civilization in which every situation is seen as a symptom of the collapse of traditional values.

THE ENDS OF TIME

A much larger cycle of time is completed in the Kali Yuga, the last and most corrupt of four consecutive ages in the Hindu Manvantara and, according to ancient tradition, the time period in which we are now living. The *Vishnu Purana* text is specific about the qualities to be associated with the Kali Yuga:

> When society reaches a stage where property confers rank, and wealth becomes the only source of virtue, passion the sole bond of union between husband and wife, falsehood the source of success in life, sex the only means of enjoyment …

then we are in the Kali Yuga, allegedly the world of today. The same text goes on to say that in these times there will be

> no one, anymore, in whom enlightening goodness prevails: no real wise man, no saint, no one uttering truth and standing by his sacred word. The seemingly holy brahmin is no

better than the fool. Old people, destitute of the true wisdom of old age, try to behave like the young, and the young lack the candor of youth.[169]

In a fascinating study called *The Reign of Quantity,* a modern scholar has further developed this Hindu tradition and expanded its teachings into the twentieth century. René Guénon not only believed that the world was approaching the end of the Kali Yuga; he also felt that the traits he identified with that particular ending were applicable to the final phase of other major cycles of time. There are, he claimed, many endings of Time, as many as there are cycles of varied duration, "contained as it were one within another,"[56] all sharing to some extent the qualities he attributes to the end of the final phase of the Hindu Manvantara.

Guénon was one of the most brilliant scholars of the twentieth century. He was also, from a Western point of view, one of the most unorthodox. Born in Blois, France, in 1886 and raised in a strict Catholic family, Guénon went as a youth to Paris to take a degree in mathematics but found himself drawn instead to the study of Eastern religions — Hinduism, Taoism, and Sufism. He moved to Egypt in 1930 and lived there until his death in 1951. Among his many scholarly books, *The Reign of Quantity* is particularly concerned with the phenomena that he believed must inevitably accompany the final phase of any cycle of time. The disorder that Guénon perceived in the twentieth century would, he believed, eventually find its place among the elements of universal order. For him, it was only the partial point of view, plucked from the context of the whole, that could seem chaotic. "Thus, whereas the modern world considered in itself is an anomaly and even a sort of monstrosity," he wrote, "when seen as the last phase of an historical cycle it is clear that the present times could not be otherwise than they actually are." And for Guénon, that last phase is marked by a disintegration of form.[56]

He found two characteristic tendencies at the ends of cycles: first, an inclination toward the solidification of the world, followed by a tendency toward its dissolution. Guénon believed that the second of these tendencies had already begun to predominate early in the twentieth century, most notably, one assumes, in the scientific domain, where solid matter was being dissolved by physicists into fields of energy and dynamic processes. In the arts of the same period, Cubism was fragmenting solid forms into their geometry (figure 16), precipitating a massive breakdown of the tradition of depicting the world in recognizable ways that was furthered by the beginnings of abstract art (figure 17).

The activities of Marcel Duchamp further dissolved the well-defined boundaries of the arts. As early as 1913 Duchamp's "readymades"—manufactured objects like snow shovels, urinals, bicycle wheels (see figure 23)—broached the idea that anything, and by extension any activity, could be considered art. One of his friends recalled Duchamp's enthusiasm as he gazed upon an airplane propeller, exclaiming, "Who will do better?"[135] A few years later (1919) Duchamp pencilled a moustache and goatee on a reproduction of the *Mona Lisa,* while the Dada movement was proclaiming the end of art itself. "What is the value of art," the Dadaists asked, "and is there any?"[159] The rest of the twentieth century was spent trying, unsuccessfully it seems, to answer these questions.

FIGURE 16. Pablo Picasso, *Man with Violin*, 1911.

Guénon could also have pointed to the dissolving of virtually all conventions of classical music early in the twentieth century. In 1909 Arnold Schoenberg wrote to Richard Strauss from Vienna, describing the pieces he had completed so far as "absolutely not symphonic, quite the opposite—without architecture, without structure. Only an ever-changing, unbroken succession of colors, rhythms, and moods."[147] The twelve-tone technique that Schoenberg was developing went on to challenge the traditional harmonic scale. A few decades later John Cage would complete the dismantling, collapsing the boundary between music and other kinds of noise, making all sound—and all silence—available as a form of music.[19]

The traditional structures of classical ballet and literature began dissolving as well early in the twentieth century. In 1905 Isadora Duncan, dancing barefoot and in loose clothing, presented her unrestricted way of moving to Russian audiences, influencing Nijinsky as well as the Russian choreographer Michael Fokine, who began revolutionizing formal ballet in Diaghilev's Ballets Russes.[30] Four years later Diaghilev's "wild Asiatic horde" electrified Parisian audiences, beginning a twenty-year assault on every artistic convention associated with theatrical dance.[164] At the same time a Berlitz English teacher in Trieste named James Joyce was giving one of his students three chapters to read of a work that would become *A Portrait of the Artist as a Young Man.* Anticipating Joyce's *Ulysses,* it dissolved conventional literary structure into the unmarked contents of consciousness, chronological but otherwise random. "It is a mosaic of jagged fragments," wrote H.G. Wells in his review of *Portrait.* "The technique is startling, but on the whole it succeeds."[42]

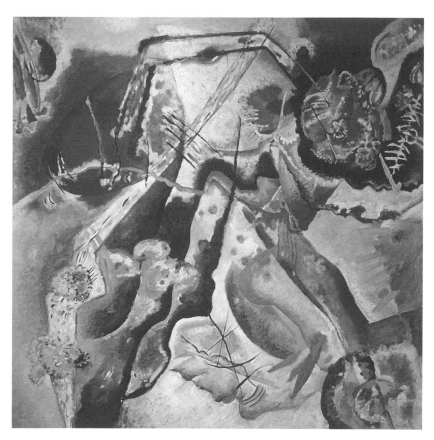

FIGURE 17. Wassily Kandinsky, *The Red Spot*, 1914.

Even the world of mathematics began to show signs of crumbling, when the mathemetician Kurt Gödel success-fully proved that every system of mathematics that man might construct is doomed to incompleteness, that the con-sistency of any formal system cannot be demonstrated within the logic of that system.[161] These instabilities, together with those described in chapter 2, seem to support Guénon's claim that the maximum solidity of stable institutions and traditions has been reached and passed, and that: "Dissolution is the goal towards which the world will be travelling henceforth."[56]

THE REIGN OF QUANTITY

For Guénon, the dissolving world necessarily finds itself subject to a "reign of quantity." He believed that a steady encroachment of quantitative values over the qualitative must inform the end-phase of a cycle:

> The descending movement of manifestation, and consequently that of the cycle of which it is an expression, takes place away from the positive or essential pole of existence towards its negative or substantial pole, and the result is that all things must progressively take on a decreasingly qualitative and an increasingly quantitative aspect; and that is why the last period of the cycle must show a very special tendency towards the establishment of a "reign of quantity."[56]

Writing before mid-century, Guénon did not live to see the development of computers and digitization, the conceptual revolution that has been criticized for draining away the qualitative nature of human experience in favor of a quantity (the binary numeric system) that it can handle.[148] Nor did he have a chance to observe the late-twentieth-century hunger for size, for ever bigger houses (three rooms larger than they were in the late seventies, though families are smaller) and cars (two-ton, four-wheel-drive "urban assault" vehicles). But he would probably not have been surprised to hear the 1980s—and we may now add the '90s as well—described as "the decade of a shameless pecuniary greed and an unchecked veneration of materialism and affluence."[82]

Chapter 3 of this book, "The World Is For Sale," might as easily have been titled "The Reign of Quantity." In a world given over to consumer capitalism, all values do seem destined to be quantitative. George Soros surprised no one in the late 1990s by advising the world to accept the fact that the dominant value in today's global capitalist system is the pursuit of money—and that publicly owned corporations, guided by management principles whose sole objective is to maximize profits, dominate economic life today as never before.[136]

Toward the end of the 1990s, which may ultimately be known as the mega-merger decade, the limits to corporate size disintegrated along with global boundaries in celebration of the value of being big. The reasoning behind most mergers seems to be that bigger companies will be more efficient—and thus more competitive—in a world of global markets and high-speed technological change. Whether or not this is true (and many economists do doubt that size is tied to efficiency or that "competition" is as important as the amassing of power),[110] the drive for size is real. Quantity, not quality, carried the late-twentieth-century day (figure 18).

On the home front, Wal-Mart, the single largest private employer in this country, led the trend toward "Brobdingnagian" chain stores with policies—"in a nutshell: lowest prices and highest product turnover equals biggest profit"[104]—that

FIGURE 18.
Andy Warhol,
*Thirty Are
Better Than One*
(*Mona Lisa*),
1963.

are everywhere accepted as guidelines to success. Collapsing many businesses into one huge one that is housed in an enormous warehouse became the 1990s ideal of retailing. Not to be outdone, banks consolidated to pioneer an age of financial superstores, defined by one critic as "the banking equivalent of one-stop shopping at the Price Club, where you can load up your gargantuan Ford Expedition sport utility vehicle with gigantic cartons of double-thick paper towels and, on the way home, stop to get your fries super-sized at McDonald's."[142]

The pressure to be bigger has affected cultural institutions like museums and concert halls as well. Success is measured by the size of their budgets, the number of programs presented, and the extent of their audiences. One art critic found the 1999 Venice Biennale geared to the quantity rather than the quality of response and concluded: "As with so much else today, the goddess of the box office stands in for blind Justice, weighing the future of art on her indifferent scales."[128] It is no secret that the music industry worships the same goddess; even contemporary classical composition is judged by how many people buy tickets.

In television, the medium whose purpose is reputedly to keep you watching long enough to see the advertisements, the number of prime-time commercials increased 33 percent between 1989 and 1998.[157] And in the movies, as Mike Nichols observes, "financial and artistic success have moved closer and closer until they're now one and the same. People talk about movies pretty much only in terms of what they grossed." Nichols makes the further point that this intensely quantitative mind-set, once generally disparaged as unworthy if not immoral, now seems perfectly natural: "When I was growing up, selling out was the big fear, it was the worst thing you could say about someone: 'Fred sold out. I'm afraid he sold out.' That doesn't even exist as an idea anymore."[110]

Live theater, which was one of the last holdouts against consolidation into the mass-audience/show-business mainstream, is now becoming "corporate theater," the latest ad-

dition to huge conglomerate families composed of movie and video studios, television and cable programmers, video-game designers, sports and music entrepreneurs, theme parks, advertising firms, news-reporting services, and publishing houses. Media empires like Time-Warner, Viacom, and News Corporation even shape the way news is presented on TV. The demand for higher ratings—bigger audiences—leads to the dramatizing of news content, making it more entertaining and upbeat lest ratings fall, sponsors are lost, and revenues slump. "The 'factual world' is thus replaced by a world constructed for entertainment and profit."[46]

The reign of quantity extends into the arts and sciences. The bigness of not only works of art (figure 19) but the new

"warehouse museums" that have been built to house such works, seems beyond artistic necessity. And the relationship of art to money has remained unchanged since Peter Schjeldahl's 1990 observation: "Money and contemporary art got married in the '80s. The couple was obnoxious and happy."[127] But two decades earlier Andy Warhol had already recognized that the principal truth about the society in which he lived was that art no longer mattered, that for a wide range of educated people, art had lost not only the old humanistic values but every other value that had ever been assigned it, "save one, which was its convertibility into cash."[156] (See figure 9.) In the sciences quality is changed into quantity on a regular basis. The prismatic colors, for example—red, orange, yellow, green, blue, indigo and violet—lose for science their quality of redness, orangeness, yellowness, etc., and become quantities, numbers expressing different frequencies of wavelengths of the vibration that we call "light."[153] In Heidegger's words: "Once you have expressed color in the form of wave-lengths, the color disappears."

THE ACCELERATION OF TIME

Guénon further believed that events unfold with increasing speed in each phase of a temporal cycle, an acceleration that becomes more exaggerated as the end of the cycle nears: "What this means is that, according to the different phases of the cycle, sequences of events comparable one to another do not occupy quantitatively equal durations."[56] He felt that as the acceleration of time became more pronounced, and change became ever more rapid, this phenomenon would seem to lead of its own accord toward dissolution.

If the acceleration of events was already perceptible in Guénon's day, how much more so is it now, a half century later, in a world outfitted with cellular phones, faxes, beepers, and e-mail? We live our lives at what seems breakneck speed, trying to keep up with events that appear to be happening even faster. Nathan Myhrwold described the rapidly accelerating rates of change in the high-tech world:

All you get is: "Bell Atlantic and TCI are going to take over the earth!" And then, "Oops, No, they're not." And: "The cable companies are King!" And: "Oops. No, the cable companies are broke!" … Striking the right balance is such a funny thing. You have this high-frequency oscillation. If you try to take a medium path through it, half the time you're a crazy Luddite. The other half the time you're a crazy optimist.[7]

It has been argued that the changing pace of media—in broadcast news, films, and especially in television shows that splice together images at fraction-of-a-second intervals—reflects, if it does not create, a change in the pace of our collective psychic life. Those who have access to a one-minute commercial from the 1950s tell us that it goes on forever: "It seems so long it's like a show."[49] In *Faster: The Acceleration of Just About Everything,* James Gleick further observes:

> As you watch the quick montages, the shotgun blasts of shots from scattered angles, you can't help but notice the pathos of the soundtracks, catering to what advertisers see as the deep concern of the audience. You hear the voices of men and women, at home and in the workplace, talking about their hectic lives, their need for time-saving, their hunger for speed. ..."[49]

In the art world, critics have observed how difficult it is to form sensible opinions about contemporary painting because of the super-rapid succession of dominant styles or movements.[161] Comparison of older and newer films of all genres shows an unmistakable quickening in the length of typical shots and in the speed of action sequences.[49] And when George Balanchine was asked to compare ballet in his time with that of the early twentieth century, he responded:

"It's a different type of dancing today. We are trained now to cover more space—faster."[30]

USING UP THE PAST

One of the most interesting of Guénon's views has to do with what he saw as the necessity of exhausting, in the final stages of a cycle, the "inferior possibilities" of ideas that were introduced earlier in the cycle—"using up everything that had been set aside in earlier periods."[56] From this point of view, the postmodern practice of reviving and imitating historical periods—the fondness of artists and architects for a pastiche of ancient and more recent styles (see figures 4 and 5)—might be interpreted as another indication that we are nearing the end of a cycle. The painter Anselm Kiefer, for example, uses historical allusions, alchemical practices, and mythological and cosmological narratives from his own Germanic tradition in his colossal, "straw-and-mud-and-blood" paintings.[51] Critics have accused Kiefer of falling into "the nostalgia trap" that has captured so much of contemporary culture, but what they see as nostalgia may actually represent a working-out of inferior possibilities of ideas introduced in earlier periods of our present cycle.

To continue this line of thought, we might note that before the late-nineteenth-century efforts of Johannes Brahms the notion of classical music apparently did not exist. The idea of a repertory of past works was of little interest to the public, who felt that for the most part "dead composers belonged on dusty shelves."[120] But Brahms, in spite of his own inventive powers, could not restrain his longing for the "golden age" of Haydn, Mozart, Beethoven, and Schubert. His activity as a manuscript editor helped to codify the work of those composers as the primary canon of musical literature, and it was only in his time that this older music began to be known and played as "classical." Although the possibilities of interpretation in the performing of these works may not yet be used up, we do seem to be trying hard.

Might the tremendous interest in archaeology also spring from an end-cycle effort to exhaust the possibilities of the past? The Dance of the Fossils is the name the cultural historian Jean Baudrillard gave to the twentieth-century desire to "unearth, uproot, and uncover every artifact produced throughout cultural history and assign it a cultural value: personal, historical, and financial."[102] Television's popular *Antiques Roadshow,* which reappraises heirlooms from the past in terms of their monetary value in today's market, offers a merger of quantitative with revivalist values that would surely have amused Guénon. Cultural recycling surfaces again in the making—or rather remaking—of movies. Who will argue that the latest version of *Psycho* is not exhausting (vastly) inferior possibilities unexplored by Hitchcock's original?

THE END OF THE WORLD

It is impossible to prove or disprove anyone's dating of the end of the Kali Yuga, the prototype for Guénon's observations. Estimates range from suspiciously concrete to unfathomably mythical numbers of years. But if we are not yet there, or even close, we are approaching the ends of other traditional cycles of time, each of which, by Guénon's reckoning, would be expected to share to some extent the qualities he describes for the last phase of the Hindu Manvantara. One of the most widely, if not always credibly, publicized of these endings is the approaching close of the "world age" associated with the constellation Pisces. And unlike the cycle of Hindu Yugas, the cycle of zodiacal ages can be fairly accurately estimated.

Because the earth is not a perfect sphere and is affected by the gravitational pull of the sun and the moon, its movement about its axis is given a twist, gradually shifting the apparent position of the sun relative to the fixed stars at the earth's equinoxes and solstices, creating what is called the precession of the equinoxes. One complete revolution of the precession takes almost 26,000 years, an era known as the Platonic, or Great, Year. In the course of one Great Year, each of the twelve constellations of the zodiac frames the rising sun at the spring equinox for approximately 2,160 years, the span of one world age.

The onset of the age of Pisces is associated by many with the birth of Christ, though various sources would move that date back or forward in time by a hundred years or so. In any case, we are to some degree approaching the end of the Piscean era, a termination that in ancient times, incidentally, may have been referred to as "the end of the world." According to one group of archaeo-astronomers, when traditional peoples spoke of the end of the world they actually meant the end of a world age, in terms of the precession of the equinoxes. When the sun no longer rose at the vernal equinox in the zodiacal constellation that had framed it for some 2,000 years, the old "world" had come to an end.[123]

There is evidence in the archaeological record to suggest that the ends of former ages also exhibited the qualities Guénon attributes to the final phase of all cycles of time. In a study of the prehistoric Mediterranean world,[129] I examined archaeological evidence of widespread cultural disintegration at around 8500 BC, which approximately marks the end of the age of the constellation Leo, and again at around 6400 BC, the approximate end of the age of Cancer in the framework of the precession of the equinoxes. In the first of these breaks, a general hiatus in settlement activity seems to have occurred throughout the Near East around the middle of the ninth millennium BC, with old settlements abandoned for an indeterminate length of time. Some 2,000 years later, another generalized break in settlement activity appears in the archaeological record, this one accompanied by visible signs of cultural decay, somewhat monstrously documented in the iconography of the Turkish site of Çatal Hüyük.

The artistic tradition at Çatal Hüyük was already dissolute when fire destroyed the settlement around 6400 BC. In the earlier study I described the unmistakable decadence revealed in the dense and overblown iconography (huge plaster wall constructions of goddesses, bulls, rams) adorning the many shrines just before the fire. The breakdown of religious distinctions was suggested by the melding and overlapping of the diverse traditions of that time within the Çatal structures. Burials in the shrines were no longer contained under platforms and had spilled out into the floor area, while less care had been taken to leave earlier burials undisturbed. This combination of carelessness and conservatism within a context of material opulence, converging cultures, and exhausted religions suggested a disintegrating society; and in fact, when Çatal Hüyük was rebuilt after the great fire, the 2,000-year-old symbolic tradition that had informed this and a great many other Near Eastern sites since around 8300 BC was nowhere in evidence.

I have not explored the increasingly complex archaeology of the late fifth and the late third millennia BC thoroughly enough to make any consistent generalizations about conditions at the ends of the ages of Gemini (c. 4200 BC) and Taurus (c. 2100 BC). But the dissolute state of Roman society at what would have been close to the end of the age of Aries (around the birth of Christ) does seem to fit this model. The cults of almost all of the foreign deities of the day—Dionysos, Isis, Mithra, Dea Syria, Kybele—had come together in Rome in a confused merging of divinities once held to be distinct. A similar breakdown was taking place in the Near East, where the collapse of the Persian Empire had dissolved all existing barriers, religious as well as political. As described by one historian:

> Heterogeneous races had suddenly come in contact with one another, and as a result [the Near East] passed through a phase of syncretism analogous to that which is more distinctly observable under the Roman Empire. The contact of all the theologies of the Orient and all the philosophies of Greece produced the most startling combinations.[32]

In *The Decline of the West,* Oswald Spengler put forth the view that every historical culture passes through a life cycle from youth to maturity, old age, and death, and he argued, like the sources mentioned earlier, that twentieth-century Western culture had entered the period of decline.[139] Spengler also gave us the idea of comparing societies that are at the same stage of their cultural cycle, regardless of their separation in time. In that sense, as I wrote in the previous study, today's declining Western civilization may be the "contemporary" of Çatal Hüyük as well as Rome. The comparison of our time to the opulence and immorality of the Roman Empire has often been made, but perhaps never so effectively as by Daniel Patrick Moynihan. When the student protests of the 1960s reached Harvard's Yard, Moynihan, who was then a member of the Harvard faculty, is said to have asked rhetorically: "Who are these people?" and offered the answer: "I suggest to you they are Christians arrived on the scene of second-century Rome."[144]

As Guénon made clear, it is only the partial view of our times that seems, to quote a previous observer, "weaselly, sordid, frightening." He assures us that in the context of the whole, of a complete historical cycle, the present time could not be other than it is. But from the perspective taken in the next chapter, the quality of this particular time may actually have as much to do with the birth of a new world as with the death of an old one.

FIGURE 20. Frank Gehry, Guggenheim Museum at Bilbao, Spain, 1998. Copyright Jeff Goldberg/Esto.

6

The World Is Beginning

Let us go then, you and I,
When the evening is spread out against the sky,
Like a patient etherized upon a table.
— T.S. Eliot, *The Love Song of J. Alfred Prufrock*

We do not belong to past dawns, but to the noons of the future.
— Aurobindo Ghose, *Message of the Gita*

If the breakdown of form that characterized the twentieth century is possibly the normal pattern for an approaching "end of a world," does it make any difference which world is ending? And which beginning? Does the fact that we are leaving the zodiacal age of Pisces and approaching that of Aquarius color the quality of our experience in any way? Ancient traditions, and many individuals today, believe that changes in celestial patterns correspond to shifts in human and terrestrial activity. For them, time is not only a measurable quantity. It has quality, and the quality of any given time on earth is believed to change along with the changes in the sky—a unity expressed by the alchemists of Renaissance Europe in the famous phrase "As above, so below."

We observed earlier that although there is no agreement about the precise date of the beginning of the Aquarian era, we are by most estimates nearing the end of the age of Pisces. And if the past 2,000-odd years have been characterized to some extent by forms and values associated with the principle of Pisces, it is those forms in particular that should be disintegrating as the Piscean age comes to an end. At the same time, we might anticipate a very different set of values beginning to emerge with the approach of the era of Aquarius, a sign that is particularly associated with revolutionary, innovative, and egalitarian ideas. From this point of view, the overturnings of tradition and the dissolving of values and distinctions may have as much to do with positive qualities associated with Aquarius as with the decay of Piscean forms. And those Aquarian qualities could be here to stay.

For example, the Piscean archetype is associated with the element of water, with the realm of emotions, feelings, and romantic imagination, with spiritual yearnings, and with an idealized and often nostalgic view of the past and its traditions. In contrast, Aquarius is associated with the element of air and particularly with the realm of the mind; its energies are said to be somewhat detached, scientific, inventive, unpredictable, and oriented to the future. Romantic novels would be considered Piscean; science fiction Aquarian. As observed by a literary critic, every major twentieth-century writer "has had to forswear whatever looked 'poetic'—flowers, romance, pets, finer feelings, neatly laced quatrains." Everything, that is, which is associated with Piscean sentiments. In the words of the poet John Ashbery: "You can't say it that way anymore."[67]

Electricity in all its forms and particularly superinnovative electronics are also a part of the Aquarian principle. It is said that as the Aquarian age approaches, our attention will

FIGURE 21. Vincent Van Gogh, *The Starry Night*, 1889.

be turned to a future influenced and dominated by the inventions of science.[61] Such a change may already be perceived in the way artists portray the night sky. According to one observer, scientific innovation has turned a cosmos that "once glittered with remote objects onto which romantic longing could be projected"[86] —as in the works of Giotto, Goya, and van Gogh (figure 21)—into a map of reachable destinations, whose craters, ice fields, and volcanic ridges have been precisely plotted (figure 22).

Inventiveness of all kinds is associated with the Aquarian archetype. In the two hundred years since the issuing of the first patents, the pace of innovation in America has acceler-

FIGURE 22. Charles Schmidt, *The Firefly: Mariner Nine's Rendezvous with Mars,* 1986.

ated until the primary source of wealth in our society has now shifted "from the business of making things to the business of thinking up things."[133] And like the world of quantum physics, technological innovation comes in unpredictable leaps. Startling developments in technology and science are constantly overtaking the vision of forecasters, while the most logical predictions are being pushed aside by the unexpected.[55] It is the unexpected and the unpredictable, as well as the scientific, that informs the principle of Aquarius.

Unpredictability has also invaded the arts, a realm traditionally associated with the spiritually inspired, idealized values of Pisces. The abrupt change in mood between the second and third lines of Eliot's *Prufrock,* written between 1910 and 1912 and quoted at the beginning of this chapter, could be read as an unexpected shift from Piscean romanticism to the irreverent, unemotional objectivity of Aquarius.

The same effect may be observed in the world of dance. In its lushly romantic and idealized beauty, classical ballet would normally be considered a Piscean experience, but what a choreographer like Balanchine did to the traditional technique in the 1970s is thoroughly Aquarian. One observer noted that in a Balanchine ballet,

> a man not only may lift his partner (as in a classical pas de deux) but may actually place her limbs in a position as if she were a puppet. Routine steps may be done with the knees turned in instead of out; a conventional pose may be shattered by the flexing of a foot usually pointed; a change of tempo or a shift of rhythmic emphasis may completely transform the quality of the movement. Gestures generally associated with emotional involvement—a stamp, a caress—are performed with a cold austerity of attack that betokens detachment, pure and heartless.[137]

From the perspective we are taking here, Balanchine's irreverent, detached, playful, essentially Aquarian choreography tweaked the classical Piscean world of dance in much the same way that Eliot's *Prufrock* had earlier done to poetry.

Every zodiacal principle is said to have both positive and negative possibilities, sometimes appearing simultaneously. Pisces, for example, is associated with all avenues of escape, from artistic and mystical transcendence to illusion (and delusion) and the abuse of drugs and alcohol. What we experience as glamorous or fashionable is also associated with the Piscean principle, through its connection to the fantasy world of dreams and longings.[52] The Aquarian principle, in contrast, operates through the medium of ideas—new ideas and new discoveries—preferably those that will improve society, as the sign is also associated with a strong social conscience. Egalitarianism is one Aquarian ideal; another, and the idea most generally identified with the archetype, is that all men should be free.

The rebellion associated with the Aquarian principle arises from a personal need to be independent and to break with convention: "a leap towards freedom, a demand for freedom, an essential movement towards an individual uniqueness."[111] As a cultural historian points out, the ideas of individualism and democracy have no definable historical connection to the growth of technology or advanced capitalism, but it's hard to imagine the development of the industrial civilization of the West without the belief in untrammelled human inquiry and the freedom to experiment, to develop, to change[22]—values that are traditionally associated with the principle of Aquarius.

These values are not dissolving. On the contrary, if measured in terms of advertising copy, the ideal (if not always the reality) of individual freedom is championed more strongly than ever. One cultural critic finds that commercial America—what he satirically calls the "businessman's republic"—is in love with the idea of revolution to a degree never before attained:

> What makes the culture of the businessman's republic so interesting is not that it demands order, conformity, gray clothes, and Muzak, but that it presents itself as an *opponent* to those very conceptions of corporate life. ... Business theory today is about revolution, not stasis or hierarchy; it's about liberation, not order. ... Business is tattooed executives

snowboarding down K2 or parachuting in hurricane weather or riding mountain bikes in tornadoes or kayaking down lava flows or running shrieking down the halls of the great bureaucracies overturning desks and throwing paper.[44]

Businessmen acting, that is, as though they are under the freedom-seeking, irreverent, unpredictable influence of Aquarius.

THE REVOLUTION OF 1910

The revolutionary inventiveness of the Aquarian mentality is perhaps most visible in twentieth-century art, where the enthusiasm for overturning tradition is exemplified in Marcel Duchamp's playful 1919 application of a moustache to a copy of the *Mona Lisa*. The early years of the century saw an explosion of invention in all the arts, sparked by a revolutionary and irreverent attitude toward the past. The shocking new dance forms introduced to Parisian society—first by Isadora Duncan in 1905 and four years later by Diaghilev's Ballets Russes—represented, from this chapter's perspective, not only a dissolving of past traditions but a revolution in innovative choreography and technique. Bold new set and costume designs for the Ballets Russes were created during the next decade by Picasso, Derain, Matisse, Juan Gris, Utrillo, and Miro, while Stravinsky, Satie, Prokofiev, and Milhaud contributed innovative musical scores in an unheard-of collaboration of the arts.[164]

Virginia Woolf once said that human nature changed in 1910.[14] Was it human nature or the quality of time that changed, reflecting a surge of revolutionary Aquarian ideas? In 1910, James Joyce was overthrowing literary traditions in the writing of *Portrait of the Artist;* T.S. Eliot, still a student at Harvard, was revolutionizing poetic convention with the etherizing of his famous patient in *Prufrock;* and Frank Lloyd Wright was designing his first Taliesin residence, a revolutionary breakthrough in the world of architecture. These were not only acts of dissolution but of intense innovation.

With the 1910 performance of his score to *Das Buch der hängenden Gärten,* Arnold Schoenberg accomplished a radical break with musical traditions, "emancipating notes from key," "liberating dissonance," and making it possible for composers to use the entire tonal spectrum in their creations.[42] For all the opposition to his innovations, Schoenberg is believed to have affected twentieth-century music more profoundly than any other person, for he had created an unrestricted tonal basis, the most revolutionary change imaginable.[84] Unless, of course, you consider American jazz—the purest musical form of improvisation and spontaneity—and its rhythmic ancestor, ragtime. In 1910 Irving Berlin was writing "Alexander's Ragtime Band," a piece that in the following year would become the most popular song in the world.[42] Jazz itself went on to redefine the relation between dissonance and consonance, melodic line and harmonic depth.[152]

And in 1910 Braque and Picasso were accomplishing a revolution in the visual arts. Their thoroughly innovative Cubist works set other artists free to explore their own paths of development, unencumbered by the traditional values of several hundred years of European painting. It was the beginning not only of the art of equally valued perspectives but of the art of ideas as well. And although Cubism is considered the philosophical equivalent of the new reality model forming in physics ("a multiplicity of frames of space, each one as good as any other"),[37] there is no question of direct influence on the painters by the scientists. Planck's quantum theory was published in 1901, but its implications were not understood until at least the 1920s, by which time all of the Cubist innovations had been made. Nor is it likely that Braque or Picasso had read Einstein's electrodynamics paper of 1905, in which he concluded that no observer had a privileged point of view. But as one analyst noted, this is not the point: "The Cubists reached their conclusions independently."[15] Were these various independent revolutions expressing an idea whose time was approaching with the Aquarian era?

After Cubism, every decade of the twentieth century offered new ideas and new ways of doing things in all the visual arts. The next and almost immediately accomplished innovation in painting involved breaking away from the attachment to an object. Even when a Cubist painting takes on all the appearances of abstraction, a known object is still the origin of the picture. At the moment this bond is broken, abstract art begins.[159] In what has been called the "moment of liberation" for Western art, painters in different places—Wassily Kandinsky in Munich, Robert Delaunay in Paris, Arthur Dove in America—began to free themselves from the representation of specific objects in any form and to move with "the force and conviction of historical necessity"[156] toward a completely abstract art. (See figure 17.)

The poet Guillaume Apollinaire, a spokesman for the Cubists, believed that the role of art in society should always be "to keep it new." Duchamp could not, it seems, do otherwise. At a time when the Cubist revolution was in danger of becoming a new orthodoxy, Duchamp kept asking the same unsettling questions about the nature of art and of reality that had led to the revolution in the first place. "I was interested in ideas—not merely in visual products," Duchamp recalled. "As early as 1913, I had the happy idea to fasten a bicycle wheel to a kitchen stool and watch it turn." With that single act (figure 23), Duchamp originated two of the most inventive approaches to modern sculpture: the "readymade" (sculpture that is made from ordinary, already existing objects) and the mobile (sculpture that involves actual movement in space).[155]

Implicit in all of Duchamp's work was the challenge to traditional concepts and definitions of art itself. As one critic observed, the aesthetic question of our time is not "What is beautiful?" but "What can be said to be art (and literature)?"[90] By establishing that anything—and by extension any activity—could be art, and by adding only a new thought, a new idea, to existing material, Duchamp's readymades served as the intellectual prototype for today's conceptual art.[135] Duchamp himself is often associated with the irreverent and playful side of the Dada movement that sprang up in Europe after World War 1 and was considered by some to represent the "desacralization of art." From the perspective we have taken here, Dadaism could be viewed instead as a radical step in the replacement of Piscean values of idealized beauty and romanticism with an Aquarian art of ideas and the unexpected.

FIGURE 23. Marcel Duchamp, *Bicycle Wheel*, New York, 1951. (Third version, after lost original of 1913.)

Aquarian qualities are everywhere evident in the course of abstract art, beginning with the work of Kandinsky and Mondrian, the fathers of the two main streams of abstract art that continued throughout the twentieth century. Kandinsky's emphasis was on freedom and individualism; his greatest gift is said to have been the demonstration that an artist can be completely free to use whatever forms and colors he pleases and to suggest with them a space of any kind that he can imagine (see figure 17). Mondrian, on the other hand, sought to discover a form of painting that would be congruent with the spirit of a scientific age (see figure 14), objectively and unemotionally laying out the underlying geometry of the universe in dynamic grids of perfectly parallel and perpendicular lines.[119, 161]

In the 1920s the Bauhaus experiment in Munich brought abstract painting into association with mechanical and chemical technology, and enterprising artists began to abandon painting altogether in favor of exploring the possibilities of the new technical media. Later, after the Bauhaus was disbanded and one of its leaders, László Moholy-Nagy, had moved to Chicago, he wrote to a friend that painting seemed out of date and insufficient at a time when new technical media were waiting to be explored: "We have now reached the stage when it should be possible to discard brush and pigment and 'paint by means of light itself.'"[161] This vision was perhaps most admirably realized in the late-twentieth-century work of James Turrell, whose magical installations are composed of empty chambers suffused with, or divided by, a radiance of colored light (figure 24).

FIGURE 24. James Turrell, *Milk Run II, 1997.*

Developments in neon tube technology gave artists a means of sculpting as well as painting with light. Invented in 1910, the neon process was originally captured by the advertising industry for use in signage, but sixty years later the sculptural possibilities of its almost ethereal luminosity could no longer be overlooked (figure 25). In the last half of the twentieth century scientific technology of all kinds played an increasingly prominent role in art until, as one critic remarked, "almost no scientific invention, principles, fact, technique, or technology seems immune to the artistic appetite."[134] In a grand survey of international art held in Germany in late 1990s, only three painters were featured

FIGURE 25. Stephen Antonakos, *Walk On Neon, 1968.*

among scores of artists. Their work was said to be "barely noticeable among the electronic Babel of chattering video screens and high-tech gear."⁹²

The use of computer technology in the arts is now so common that it is no longer considered avant garde. The language of this new art world includes expressions like "recursive chaotic algorithms" and "digital genetics," and its citizens come from every medium—painting, sculpture, architecture, dance, engineering, film. "The roiling debates, the examples and counterexamples of digital styles, give off the distinct whiff of history in the making."[93] Two artists working the Cyberware WB4, a high-end, full-body scanner, are creating images in which the body becomes an infinitely variable topography. What initially excited these artists, according to one, was the idea of simultaneity:

> the way you can see the figure from all different angles at one time … It went back for us to Cubism. But what has become so mesmerizing is that the process is sculptural and yet, because it's all done on computer, it has become so abstract that the work is like pure idea.[93]

From Duchamp to digital art, the twentieth century seems to have been defined by an increasing—Aquarian?—emphasis on ideas and technological innovation.

"COMPUTERS FOR THE PEOPLE!"

If, as some maintain, the brightest side of American history is the persistent spread of egalitarianism,[165] this particularly Aquarian ideal was given a boost by the pluralistic, democratizing urge of the 1960s. The breakdown of boundaries that once kept high and low culture apart may be seen as part of this anti-elite, egalitarian tide, as may the liberating potential of computer technology and its participatory aspects. The first personal computer revolutionaries saw what they were doing as a way of opening up and truly democratizing society.[148] From this perspective, the cry "Computers for the people!" qualifies as Aquarian through both its electronic and its egalitarian associations.

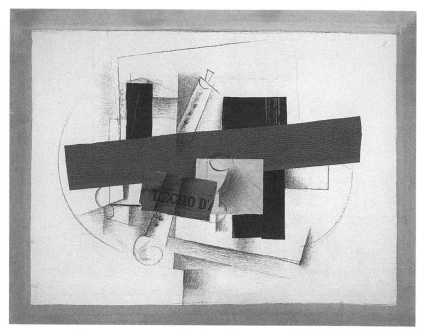

FIGURE 26. Georges Braque, *Still Life with Tenora* (formerly called *Clarinet*), 1913.

Even before the rise of the personal computer, early hackers and hobbyists were more interested in playing with new ideas than in amassing corporate profits. The concept of open-source software dates back to that time and was further refined by the efforts of Richard Stallman, a legendary hacker at MIT whose nonprofit organization promotes the use of free software. Stallman was among the influences behind Linus Torvalds' creation of Linux, an operating system that freely releases its "source code," the usually secret DNA of a computer program, on the Internet for anyone to see, modify, or redistribute. The idea of shared open-source software may indeed be "akin to the notion of Coca-Cola publishing its formula for Coke,"[57] but its egalitarian implications are classically Aquarian.

POSTMODERN EQUALITIES

An anti-elite attitude continued to surface in the arts as well, particularly in pop art, a movement whose roots can be traced back to the 1910s when Braque and Picasso began using bits of newspaper and other references to popular culture as collage elements (figure 26). In the 1960s, Andy Warhol's photomechanically reproduced images of Coke bottles and Campbell's soup cans took this populist theme to its most obvious extreme. Warhol, Tom Wesselmann, and other pop artists extended the lineage of Duchamp and the Dadaists in challenging the unique status of the art image and its elevated mystique, opening the world of art to mass culture and vice versa. (See figures 3, 7, 18.)

From the perspective taken here, postmodernism would seem to have been a natural, if radical, next step in the encroachment of Aquarian values on the Piscean territory of the arts. Some critics find that the use of elements from the past in postmodern art and architecture is not "revivalist" in the strict sense because it is done with irony, whimsy, and disbelief,[18] qualities that are also congruent with Aquarian irreverence. (See figures 4, 5.) Writing in *Commentary*, Joseph Epstein included in his definition of postmodernism "a strong reliance on irony which the advocates of postmodernism find a refreshing and fair exchange for spirituality in art."[41] Much postmodern art is also concerned with social and political issues (see figures 6, 8), an involvement that some believe should be the primary purpose of art in our time.

Similarly Aquarian qualities challenge the primacy of emotional response, a cherished value in the Piscean world. Postmodern art usually carries a certain manner or quality of utterance and performance—"deadpan, indifferent, depersonalized, effaced"—that obliterates the possibility of a conventional emotional reaction from the audience.[83] This kind of affect-free aesthetic quality can be found in the minimalist musical compositions of Steve Reich or Philip Glass and the prose fiction of Thomas Pynchon. If this detached attitude reflects an Aquarian insistence on an unemotional approach to the arts, the sentimentality that colors much of so-called New Age art may actually belong to the old age.

Aquarian tendencies are on display in contemporary dance as well. What Balanchine did in the 1970s to classical ballet was described earlier, while modern dance was energized from its early-twentieth-century beginnings by the drive to continually invent itself anew. When the radical innovations of Martha Graham and Doris Humphrey had been exhausted in the 1950s, another revolution was immediately at hand. One of the first to break away was Merce Cunningham, who left behind dependence on plot and character portrayal and began looking for purely objective ways of composing human movement.[137] Beginning not with feeling but with movement itself, he then sought out music that could not be interpreted emotionally. Working with John Cage, Cunningham arranged his dances independently of Cage's music, without reference to the accompanying sound patterns, to make certain there was no subjective influence. His choreography was thus "autonomous; free of drama, free of music."[30] Free, that is, of elements traditionally associated with the Piscean principle.

Alwin Nikolais, for whom the major characteristic of contemporary dance is freedom, also sought to rid his dances of any expression of personal emotion. Because of their lack of literal associations, sounds created on electronic tape were often used for Nikolais' choreography, guaranteeing the unpredictability of what was to come. Egalitarian principles were prominent: men and women in Nikolais' company invariably wore the same kinds of costumes, which had been designed to minimize sexual differences or to eliminate them entirely. Even lifting and carrying were not the exclusive tasks of men, and contacts between the dancers, though physical, were impersonal.[132] As a critic observed of Nikolais' choreography: "The important thing was not to limit movement design by insisting that it represent emotions."[30]

Both Cunningham and Nikolais used technically skilled dancers, but other choreographers chose to free themselves from even this convention. In the 1960s, performance groups associated with the Judson Dance Theater experimented with nondancers making ordinary movements that anyone in the street could do. By using people who had no particular dance skills, these choreographers set up a new kind of egalitarian relationship between the performer and the audience: "they became peers."[30] Rejected was the mystique that traditionally prevailed in the relationship between artist and audience. The groups' use of sports, games, tasks, and "perambulations" (a young Robert Rauschenberg performed there on roller skates) raised the audience's taste for playful unpredictability—and raised again, for dance, the question of what can be called art.

If the individuals named above seem to embody Aquarian qualities, the work of a successful contemporary choreographer like Lars Lubovitch suggests that the values of the Piscean age are still with us as well. In assessing Lubovitch's work, a critic points out:

> While many of his colleagues soberly explore social ills or, fascinated by formal concerns, coolly toy with the limits of dance itself, much of his work is lushly romantic, passionate, tender, full of dazzling, ribbonlike curves, eye-confounding lifts and spins, swirling ensembles that part, regather and part again. In a time when beauty is deeply suspect in all the arts, Lubovitch's work is frankly, shamelessly beautiful.[108]

Lubovitch himself is quoted as saying: "People come down hard on you for subscribing to romanticism, passion, sentimentality, guilelessness—to representations of beauty in a traditional sense."[108]

Why is that? Is it because, like the ban on flowery poetry mentioned earlier, "you can't say it that way anymore"? And which people come down hard on romanticism? Probably not the wider dance audience of today, which is still finding its way into dance performances through cues associated with musical or verbal theater.[132] It's difficult for these onlookers to identify with Merce Cunningham, much less with the work of his students like Mark Morris, in part because these choreographers are about pure movement rather than the romantic expressiveness that characterizes most other theater. Nostalgia for traditional forms of beauty is a powerful—and powerfully Piscean—force, and artistic values of the past may continue to be revived until their exhaustion is complete.

Throughout the twentieth century, nostalgia has been expressed as a longing for a return to a world of order, meaning, and solidarity. Many people today believe and hope that the changes all around them represent only a temporary crisis, that sooner or later we will find our way back to the old ways of life and all present symptoms will be eradicated, like a debilitating disease that will finally be healed. But another observer thinks differently, and sets the stage for the evolutionary perspective of the next chapter:

> People of greater insight know, to the contrary, that there can be no return to the old times and that it is senseless to try to turn back the wheel of evolution. They know that what matters most is that this new man come into the world healthy and vigorous.[81]

FIGURE 27. Pablo Picasso, *Portrait of Ambroise Vollard*, 1910.

7

The World Is Evolving

Now, more than hitherto, there occur shocks, surges, crossings,
falls, and almost scrambles, creating thus a different space,
a space scattered and unknown, space enclosing spaces,
superimposed, inserted, polyphonic perspectives.
—Henri Michaux, *Emergences, resurgences*

From another point of view, what we are referring to as the dissolution of form may actually be the disintegration of an outworn mode of human consciousness. For cultural philosopher Jean Gebser, the destruction of familiar realities and the multiplying of perspectives in our time is caused, not by our position at the end or the beginning of a cycle of time, but by the impact of an emergent mode of awareness that he calls the integral structure of consciousness.

Gebser was a scholarly Eastern European expatriate who eventually settled in Switzerland to record his insights on the structure and evolution of human consciousness, most accessibly in *The Ever-Present Origin* (1949). Although he probably never met René Guénon, the two men shared a concern over the dominance of quantitative values in our time. But whereas Guénon attributed the "reign of quantity" to our position at the end of a cycle of time, Gebser viewed it as an indication of the fatigue of our present mental-rational structure of consciousness: "The exhaustion of a consciousness structure has always manifested itself in an emptying of all values, with a consistent change of efficient qualitative to deficient quantitative values."[45]

Gebser saw human consciousness as an evolution, an unfolding through five historical stages that he termed archaic, magical, mythical, mental-rational, and (now emerging) integral structures of consciousness. Each of these modes of consciousness determines how the world was experienced and understood during the period of its dominance. Magical consciousness perceived events as the operation of occult or uncanny forces; mythical consciousness sought meaning through grand images and stories of the gods; mental consciousness, our present structure, searches for rational understandings. The incoming integral consciousness allows, as the name implies, the free expression of all of the other structures without being captured by any of them.[31] According to Gebser, the so-called expansion of consciousness that has received so much publicity in the twentieth century is actually "a spatially conceived quantification of consciousness and consequently an illusion."[45] What we are dealing with instead, he wrote, is an *intensification* of consciousness that is inclusive of all previous structures.

As Gebser's interpreters point out, we need only look around us to find examples of individuals still translating reality in terms of each of these earlier modes of consciousness. In religious contexts, for example, there are people practicing shamanism and other forms of magic, while some of the world's oldest organized religions worship mythical concepts of gods and goddesses, and theologians argue in mental-rational terms about ethics and the nature of God.[31] But a new coalition of these structures of consciousness is also observable in our time. The concept of "action at a distance," which was fundamental to a magical way of seeing the world, today permeates the mental-rational realms of quantum theory, as does the idea that reality is indivisible. "Magic offered a blueprint of a unified world in which division—and therefore alienation—was impossible. This blueprint, which had no more substance than a dream, now has become a scientific aim."[15]

The mythic consciousness structure has also penetrated our mental-rational world, most notably perhaps in the elevation of the feminine principle—frequently associated with veneration of the Goddess—within an American culture otherwise dominated by what has been referred to as "male reductionist rationality." Increased interest in Jungian psychology and Joseph Campbell's studies of myth may also be considered part of this late-twentieth-century resurgence of the mythic mode of consciousness. The circular or cyclic image of time and the idea of correspondence between changes in the night sky and the patterns of human existence belong to the mythic structure as well.

In fact, from Gebser's perspective the book you are reading might be seen as a combination of all three modes of consciousness, offering a magical point of view in the invisible web of energies described in chapter 4 and a mythical perspective in the cycles and qualities of time explored in chapters 5 and 6, with an overall rational structure keeping the others in line. In any case, the earlier chapter on capitalism seems a fair description of where an exclusively mental-rational point of view has taken the world. What matters most in the main stream of Western culture is, as Gebser put it, "still the valueless facts, the material and rational."[45]

The Western mentality has tended to assume that ways of knowing from the past must be inferior to the rational intellect. But the postmodern movement, and the 1960s counterculture from which it emerged, are now being recognized as part of a larger chorus of "revolutionary cries for liberation from the constraints—intellectual, social, and sexual—of a narrowly rationalist modernity."[18] Walter Truett Anderson has written extensively about the limitations of the eighteenth-century Enlightenment ideal of a universal culture built on a foundation of rational thought. In 1995 Anderson concluded that the individual mind may actually be pluralistic in itself, "naturally predisposed to function in many modes."[4] For Gebser, those modes would be the magical, mythic, and mental; and the predisposition to function effectively in all of them would indicate the emergence of the integral structure of consciousness.

The thinking of Gregory Bateson, who in chapter 4 gave us the image of driving both Lake Erie and ourselves crazy, may exemplify Gebser's ideal of integral consciousness. Bateson considered the Enlightenment view of man as the conquerer of nature to be utterly unscientific. His own way of knowing was based, in the words of one of his students, "on the lessons of myths, the wisdom of the 'primitive,' and the archaic algorithms of the heart."[16] Bateson's stance was not in opposition to the rational intellect, but only to its inability to locate itself in a larger context. Like Gebser, he realized that the price to be paid for operating exclusively out of the mental-rational mode is a failure to perceive the whole.

This fundamental inadequacy of the mental structure of consciousness might be compared to the inability of mechanistic Newtonian physics to describe the reality that is indicated by quantum theory. But just as we still use Newton's laws in dealing with the everyday world, there is no question of abandoning the rational mind in favor of the magic or mythical. Gebser warned that it is not uncommon for the anxiety caused by the fragmenting of a given consciousness structure to generate reversions to earlier modes, modes that promise salvation from the ravages of the dissolving structure. In the present transition from the mental to the integral, efforts to retreat to the earlier mythic mode of consciousness may take the form of fierce nationalism or religious fundamentalism, while regression to the magical structure could manifest as drug or alcohol abuse.[77]

THE ERUPTION OF TIME

For Gebser, the most conspicuous sign of the emergence of the integral consciousness structure is the time-anxiety of our era. As early as the beginning of the twentieth century, the mental-rational structure of consciousness began to be challenged by what he called the "eruption of time," time emerging as an intensity or quality. Earlier, the eruption of space—the discovery of perspectivity in the Renaissance—had led to the rationalism and quantification that characterized Enlightenment thought. But Gebser suggested that even as those rational tendencies were increasing, a counterforce could be detected that in the early years of the twentieth century "entered the disintegrating world of the mental-rational consciousness with great momentum."[43] This force was atemporality, the awareness of time as significantly more fundamental to our being than is suggested by its measured division into past, present, and future.

Atemporality integrates spatial perspectives, allowing one to see something from all sides at once, omnipresent, "aperspectival." In the mental-rational mode, time and space are separate entities; time is linear and measured in the language of space. But thinking of present time as "in-betweenness," something lying between past and future, is a perversion, claimed Gebser, who saw time as a basic constituent of space: "not a part of space, that is, a disqualified dimension, but its very basis and basic dimension." As soon as time and space are perceived as a continuum, as Einstein accomplished early in the twentieth century, time is recognized as the "fundamental constituent of the world ... immeasurable and not amenable to rational thought."[45]

Understanding the idea of an atemporal and aperspectival consciousness is made more difficult by the mental-rational language of today. Other, more useful modes of expression have begun to proliferate across disciplines, and concepts of "indeterminacy," "probability," and "chaos" could indicate an eruption of nonlinear time. The Zen master, on the other hand, tries to overcome the Western language bias by keeping his words on the subject as simple as possible:

> Here there is no idea of time or space. Time and space are one. You may say, "I must do something this afternoon," but actually there is no "this afternoon." We do things one after the other. That is all. There is no such time as "this afternoon" or "one o'clock" or "two o'clock." At one o'clock

you will eat your lunch. To eat lunch is itself one o'clock. You will be somewhere, but that place cannot be separated from one o'clock. For someone who actually appreciates our life, they are the same.[146]

For those convinced of the exclusive validity of the rational consciousness, Gebser warned that the eruption of time must seem the ultimate destroyer of realities that were once deemed secure. But this eruption is destructive only if we fail to comprehend what time actually is. If we are able to realize that "time" includes each of the ways of perceiving time that accompanied the previous structures of consciousness—including what Gebser has called "the presence of origin"—we experience liberation rather than the loss of security. He further believed that it is only by recognizing that we are actually composed of all forms of time that we can be freed from our exclusive attachment to mental-linear time: "The courage to accept along with the mental time concept the efficacy of pre-rational magic timelessness and irrational mythical temporicity makes possible the leap into arational time freedom."[45]

The British author J.B. Priestley, describing himself as a time-haunted man, referred to our present linear, quantified concept of time as "the worst idea of Time men have ever had."[114] According to Gebser, few of us are aware of the immeasurable loss of freedom imposed by the quantifying of time. We have become addicted to overcoming time by "saving" it, not only through telecommunications and supersonic aircraft but by medical attempts to extend human longevity. "Precisely these exertions, fleeing into quantification, are a temporal flight born of the time-anxiety which dominates our daily lives." But to be haunted by time is also to approach integral consciousness: "Only man today who is now awakening or mutating toward the aperspectival consciousness takes note of every hour of his apparent lack of time that drives him to the brink of despair."[45]

Gebser saw two ways of reacting to the uncertainty and confusion in the world around us. The first and most common is to feel alienated, destabilized, and helpless; the second is to recognize the open quality of the world and sustain it through our own openness. This open world becomes plenitude, he claimed, "whenever we realize that the disruption of space by time does not lead to emptiness or nothingness but to transparency."[45]

Gebser's use of the word "transparency" predates its popularity in today's diplomatic and trade circles, where it has become a catchword for the openness of political operations to the public gaze. Gebser used it (alternately with the unwieldy word "diaphaneity") to characterize the power of the integral structure of consciousness to lay open the reality of both self and world. The integrating of the constituent aspects of man—the magic, mythic, and mental structures of which he is composed—requires that these forms become transparent and conscious within the individual: "Only as a whole man is man in a position to perceive the whole."[45]

The world outside the individual then becomes open to his gaze. The transparency associated with the integral mode of consciousness manifests as a "seeing through," or becoming aware of, the essential qualities of the things of the world.[160] We have mentioned the indebtedness of early-twentieth-century artists to Cézanne in their efforts to paint the essence rather than the appearance of an object. When Cézanne painted the teacup as if it were living, he was seeing through the surfaces to its essential quality—perhaps something like Plato's "idea" of a teacup. As observed by an art historian: "Before Cézanne, every painting was to some extent like a view seen through a window. Courbet had tried to open the window and climb out. Cézanne broke the glass. The room became part of the landscape, the viewer part of the view."[15] This is transparency.

EARLY MULTIPLE PERSPECTIVES

In *The Ever-Present Origin,* Gebser documented ways in which the fields of physics, mathematics, biology, sociology, and philosophy as well as the arts have struggled with the eruption of time. From his point of view, the common effort—conscious or not—among these disciplines has been to overcome their exclusively rational approaches and "to perceive the world freely, universally, and to a certain extent from all sides," including the view into the interior.[45]

In the field of physics, for example, the eruption of time was experienced early in the twentieth century, when Einstein demonstrated that space, which had been considered timeless, was actually inseparable from motion, which involves time. The measurement of time and space was found to depend on where you are and how fast you and they are going when you measure them. According to the quantum mechanics of the 1920s, a wave from one point of view was, when seen from another perspective, a particle; what was field in one experiment was trajectory in the next. In the words of one observer: "Physics could only be rescued from permanent anomaly by Niels Bohr and his principle of complementarity, which essentially turned the double point of view into a new law of nature."[42]

Meanwhile, Braque and Picasso were exploring the idea that an object cannot truly be seen from only one perspective, creating composite images that were painted as if viewed from many different angles at once. (See figures 1, 2, 10, 16 and 27.) In this effort they were again following the example of Cézanne, who first introduced the idea that a painting can have multiple points of view. In his *Still Life with Basket* (figure 28), the basket of fruit is seen simultaneously from different angles: the top from above, the side of the basket from a level gaze. In Gebser's model this simultaneous presentation of multiple perspectives, carried further by the Cubists, is an expression of the integral consciousness structure. And again like Cézanne, the Cubists were striving for transparency, seeking to "penetrate the object and divulge its interior, making this view copresent with all parts."[160]

Points of view began to multiply in early-twentieth-century literature as well, particularly through the use of irony, said to be the literary equivalent of the Cubist way of painting and of multiple exposure in photography. With irony, an observer points out, it is possible to "speak one's piece in more than one tone of voice."[42] Linear concepts of time were also under siege, with mythic consciousness given its literary due. Reviewing Joyce's *Ulysses,* T.S. Eliot wrote: "In

FIGURE 28. Paul Cézanne, *Still Life with Basket*, 1888–1890.

using the myth, in manipulating a continuous parallel between contemporaneity and antiquity, Mr. Joyce is pursuing a method which others must pursue after him."[138] Eliot had already followed his own advice in writing *The Waste Land*, a contemporary poem that is constructed on ancient and modern mythic parallels and consistently takes place in both the present and the past.

Along with physics, literature, and the visual arts, the music of the early twentieth century erupted with inclusive perspectives on time. Since the seventeenth century, musical time had been divided into more or less regular pulse, 3 or 4 beats to a measure or some variation thereof. With the music of Arnold Schoenberg, time was freed from classical constraints. Schoenberg's atonality is said to correspond to a time sense that is different from and incompatible with those of all previous modes of music: "Therefore atonal music represents a new type of symbolic time."[147] Simultaneously with Schoenberg's advances but on the other side of the Atlantic, the music called ragtime was on piano stands by 1908. Ragtime meant what its name implied: tearing up the standard 4/4 or 3/4 pop music beat into smaller bits of time, not always equal in size, and sewing them together again to allow polyrhythm and syncopation.[42]

In architecture, time is expressed in movement, in the dynamics of space. When Frank Lloyd Wright began tearing down walls to allow space to flow freely, the result was a merging of the once-distinct perspectives of time and space. The time-space continuum being explored by Wright's contemporaries in physics was independently becoming the "style" of an architect who had freed himself of any one style and worked instead with the penetration of light. The open quality of Wright's structures allows a simultaneous viewing of interior and exterior, which in turn produces the effect of transparency, one space seen through the other.[160]

POSTMODERN ART

Gebser's concept of integral consciousness anticipated by several decades the spread of postmodern sensibilities in Western culture, but he would not have been surprised at the definition of postmodernism as "what happens when the restless doubting attitude of modern reason turns on reason itself."[89] In calling into question the fruits of modern rationalism, the antirational protests of the postmodernists picked up the thread pulled earlier in the century by Marcel Duchamp and the Dadaists. From the perspective taken here, this lineage of protest previews the shift from an exclusively mental-rational to an integral structure of consciousness.

One of the basic themes of postmodernism has to do with a plurality of perspectives, expressed by artists through the use of collage, pastiche, and multiple video devices. The work of Nam June Paik was chosen by one critic as illustrative of what today's artist may ask of the observer in this regard. Frequently Paik's artistic materials consist of stacked or scattered television screens that recapitulate prearranged sequences of images at unsynchronized moments on the various screens:

> An older aesthetic is then practiced by viewers who, bewildered by this discontinuous variety, decide to concentrate on a single screen, as though the relatively worthless image sequence to be followed there had some organic value in its own right. The postmodernist viewer, however, is called upon to do the impossible, namely, to see all the screens at once, in their radical and random difference.[65]

Is what is asked here of the viewer truly impossible, or does this installation require instead an integral, aperspectival, consciousness?

In postmodern painting the past and its traditions serve simply as other perspectives. The contemporary artist Robert Rauschenberg speaks of introducing "the past into the present, totality into the moment."[161] In *Tracer* (figure 29) he juxtaposes Rubens' *Venus Before the Mirror* with an American eagle, floating cubes, helicopters, and a Manhattan street scene. Other postmodern artists have gone still further in integrating the mythical and archaic into their work; the paintings of German artist Anselm Kiefer in particular are said to uncover the "enigmatic density of images that hark back to ancient ways of thinking long repressed."[48]

As mentioned earlier, the difficulty in understanding the idea of an atemporal and aperspectival consciousness is due in part to the mental-rational bias in our language. The surfacing of more useful concepts—probability, indeterminacy, chaos—was also noted earlier and is nowhere more powerfully displayed than in the worlds of contemporary music and dance. John Cage made indeterminacy the organizing principle of his music, using "chance operations" in compositions that welcome accidental sounds from the surroundings or from electronic devices.[19] In his *Europeras 1 and 2* the main scene was formed of a combination of fragments of opera that were no longer subject to copyright, music scores that had been photocopied at random, arbitrary stage backdrops, and sets that moved in random time, with a computer program compiled by chance operations controlling the lighting process. Cage then proceeded to add his own elements, weaving visual jokes and puns into twelve alternate plots, "thus creating a beguiling and entertaining pastiche of cultural productions of the past as a gaming collage for the present."[87]

In postmodern dance, antirational elements replaced linear story lines while chance and improvisation overturned

FIGURE 29. Robert Rauschenberg, *Tracer*, 1963.

traditional concepts of cause and effect. For example, the choreographer Merce Cunningham isolated the actions performed by various parts of the human body, wrote each on a separate slip of paper, and without looking, drew the order of their appearance in his dances. He used chance again to determine the direction and duration of otherwise consciously composed movements. According to one dance critic: "With such manipulation, even a quite common movement takes on an extraordinary quality as it is done slower or faster than usual."[137] Like his friend Cage, Cunningham gave stillness its own time value and made it a positive element in his work. For these men, as for Gebser, time had quality and intensity and was a basic constituent of space.

The architects Frank Gehry (see figure 20) and Daniel Libeskind qualify as a next generation in the line of dynamic unpredictability that runs the course of the twentieth century from Duchamp to Cage to Cunningham. Libeskind is a musician, poet, and philosopher as well as an enthusiastic student of chaos theory. His design for the extension of London's Victoria and Albert Museum (figure 30) is superbly "chaotic," replacing the linear and logical with the nonlinear and complex. Unlike a classic spiral that moves around a stationary center in regularly expanding orbits, the center of Libeskind's spiral shifts, and "its orbits jump." The absence of rectilinear space is characteristic of Libeskind's work, and in the Victoria and Albert design he abandons the level planes of modern architecture's upright boxes—as well as the more conventional spiral form of Frank Lloyd Wright's New York Guggenheim—in favor of an unpredictable and dynamic irregularity. "The world," observed Libeskind, "is

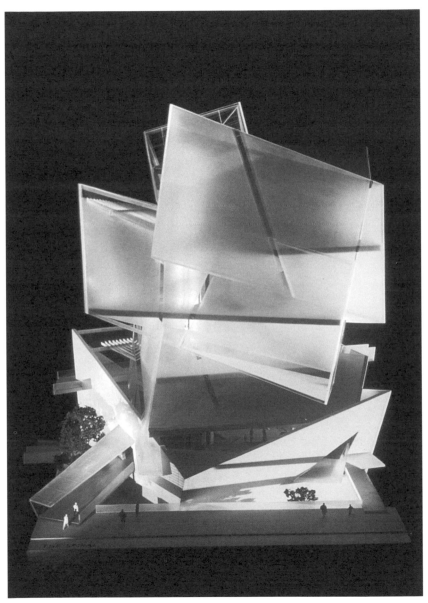

FIGURE 30. Daniel Libeskind, "Spiral" building, the original model for the 1996 competition for an extension to the Victoria and Albert Museum, London.

based on mysteries ... everything cannot be reduced to the rational."[103] Would Gebser see in his work an architectural demonstration of integral consciousness?

FUNDAMENTAL REALITY

Gebser's vision of the evolution of human consciousness is not an easy one to grasp, and I urge readers not to rely on my understanding of this complex scheme but to track down a copy of *The Ever-Present Origin* and put together their own interpretations. Scholars have spent lifetimes struggling to assimilate Gebser's ideas, which are no more or less challenging than other models of consciousness evolution proposed in this century by Rudolf Steiner, Aurobindo Ghose, or Pierre Teilhard de Chardin, models that incidentally are in many ways surprisingly similar—and similarly difficult. The subject seems inevitably to be as complicated as it is compelling. As the twentieth century has been designated by all of these evolutionary theorists as the beginning of a critical shift in human consciousness, we may perhaps hope that the new consciousness structure will include the ability to fully comprehend its evolution.

In the meantime, more accessible cultural observers have presented us with related views of the meaning of this time for human development. Walter Truett Anderson, for example, argues that true progress, both human and cultural, has little to do with the kind of material well-being that comes with the creation of more goods and services, greater mobility, or high-tech wonders. His idea of authentic progress in many ways resembles an evolution of consciousness: "an

FIGURE 31. George Segal, *Portrait of Sidney Janis with Mondrian Painting*, 1967.

ever-increasing reflexivity" in which each era of history sees previous eras as well as itself, and the individual mind becomes ever more able to think about its own thought.[5] (See figure 31.) An enthusiastic postmodernist, Anderson maintains that all explanations of reality are human constructions, useful but not perfect, and he considers the primary achievement of the postmodern period to be the ability to "step out of" any given construct, and see it as such.

Anderson acknowledges the prior existence in other cultures of a recognition of the illusory nature of reality. For him, what is new at this time is the pervasiveness of such ideas throughout the world and the willingness of so many people to state them openly: "For the first time, things are happening to the entire human species at once."[5] It is true that from the times of Plato and the Hindu Vedanta to the present, the idea that the world of appearances is an illusion has been repeatedly affirmed by the mystics of every tradition. What they also affirmed, however, was the very unpostmodern idea that behind this illusory construct lies a hidden, implicit, and more fundamental reality.

The belief in an underlying reality is intrinsic to the work of Gebser and other theorists of the evolution of consciousness, but mainstream Western science still tends to regard such ideas as farfetched. As sketched in chapter 4, however, a body of recent scientific thought is moving in a direction that is consistent with the idea of a more basic reality than our everyday model. "We have reached a stage," writes one observer, "at which a physicist like David Bohm can speak of an implicate order, hidden beneath the web of things and relations that we observe, without being expelled from the scientific community."[29]

None of the cultural philosophers mentioned here believes that the anticipated changes will happen without great difficulty. Gebser himself warns that the shift from the mental-rational to the integral structure of consciousness will be tremendously challenging. But he goes on to say:

The more the manifestations of our age of transition and decline make known their desperate and furious struggle, the greater will the vitality and intensity of the new, world-transforming manifestations stand out.[45]

For Gebser, any attempt to foresee the shaping of the future in "time" can only be illusory, since he believes the present form of time will end with the newly emerging integral consciousness. One of his interpreters, however, suggests that unless a major regressive trend sets in, we may expect perspectives and opinions in all realms of culture to continue becoming more fluid and playful, while conservative factions resist these trends "as if their very existence were threatened to its roots, as indeed it is."[31]

FIGURE 32. Yves Klein, *Untitled blue monochrome*, 1960, 76¾ x 55¼ inches.

8

The World Is

One of the most interesting aspects of quantum theory is the fact that there are many different and mostly contradictory interpretations of what the theory "really means," and all of them are accurate. That is, they all accurately explain the behavior of known experiments and correctly predict the results of new experiments.[53] Heinz Pagels explored this enigma, and in *The Cosmic Code* this eminent physicist advised his colleagues to learn a little about the quantum world from each of the different interpretations, viewing all of them together in a kind of "superposition of possibilities."[107]

Few physicists have followed Pagels' lead, choosing instead to believe that their preferred interpretation is right and all others wrong. Yet these scientists should be more familiar than the rest of us with the work of Kurt Gödel and Niels Bohr, who showed that it is impossible to arrive at any set of fundamental axioms that is complete and unambiguous in itself (Gödel), and that reality is irreducibly complex and plural, unable to be exhausted by any single theoretical description and needing instead various languages and perspectives (Bohr).

In the same situation Nietzsche might have done better. More than one hundred years ago, Friedrich Nietzsche realized that reality was too complex and many-sided to be grasped from a single perspective.[19] He was one of the first to advocate looking at the world through many lenses, believing that the more perspectives one had at one's disposal, the better one could understand phenomena. Nietzsche was once criticized by a friend for being able to adopt any standpoint at will and for boasting of what his friend saw as a defect: "freedom from any compulsion to see the world in any particular light."[62]

It was Nietzsche's claim that the cultivation of multidimensional seeing, rather than a fixed "philosophy," would enable one to respond more appropriately to each situation in life:

> We usually endeavor to acquire a single deportment of feeling, a single attitude of mind toward all the events and situations of life—that, above all, is what is called being philosophically minded. But for the enrichment of knowledge it may be of more value not to reduce oneself to uniformity in this way, but to listen instead to the gentle voice of each of life's different situations; these will suggest the attitude of mind appropriate to them.[105]

What Nietzsche did not accept, however, was the possibility that some of life's situations might require metaphysical attitudes of mind. He took pride, as have so many intellectuals of the twentieth century, in his staunchly antimetaphysical conception of the world. Such a stance suggests, however, that his own view might never be more than partial, that Nietzsche was unable, after all, to master *every* perspective.

Can we? Following the chapter titles, can we really see the world as simultaneously for sale, alive, ending, beginning, and evolving? To be open, genuinely open, to all points of view is hard. Many of you probably felt resistance to one or more of the perspectives I've described. For a long time the zodiac was my own area of dissent, but when I began to study the archaeology of the ancient world and saw how many advanced cultures had taken seriously the idea of correspondences between heavenly and earthly events, I began to question my uneducated bias. Eventually I concluded that this very old tradition has been corrupted by time, and that the daily horoscope in my newspaper has little to do with the principles of its ancestor. I still don't understand how it works; I'm not sure anyone does; but as J.B. Priestley once said, "If the idea that we are living at the end of the Pisces era of the Great Year adds a touch of wonder and mystery to our lives, then so much the better."[114]

This brief collection of perspectives is obviously only a sampling of the possible ways one could look at our time. Some of these views appear to be complementary: consumer capitalist ideology seems a near-perfect fit with both the "reign of quantity" that Guénon found typical of the ends of cycles of time and the shift to quantitative values that Gebser expected to accompany the exhaustion of a consciousness structure. Other perspectives appear to be contradictory: the allegedly incoming Aquarian principle is generally associated with realms of the mind, but in Gebser's evolutionary model, the mental consciousness structure is about to be superceded. It is possible, of course, that the meaning of "mind" in the Aquarian era could eventually turn out to be something more like Gebser's new integral structure, which is said to include the mental-rational along with earlier modes of consciousness. This apparent contradiction might also be resolved by studying other evolutionary theorists' descriptions of the approaching shift of consciousness: Rudolf Steiner's consciousness soul, Sri Aurobindo's supramental realm, or William Irwin Thompson's planetary consciousness.

Or we might want to leave the contradictions intact. The new science of chaos and change is actively pursuing the idea that the ways to see what nature is doing may be both multiple *and* contradictory, that reality is actually a matter of "endless nuance."[23] The philosopher Odo Marquard also prizes contradiction, but for a different reason. From his point of view, one cultivates a multitude of perspectives not only to better approach reality but to remain free of any one of them, to protect oneself from "the sole determining clutches of a single power." Marquard's essay *In Defense of the Accidental* urges us to hold fast to contradictory convictions, convictions that collide with one another in such a way that each declines in power and leaves the individual free:

The principle is: *"Divide et fuge!"* (Divide and escape!) Thus it is advantageous for man, because of the consequences in terms of freedom, to have many convictions: not no convictions at all, and not only one, but many. And it is advantageous for him to have many traditions and stories, and also many souls (alas!) in his own breast: not no tradition, story, or soul at all, and not only one, but many.⁹⁵

What makes a human being free, Marquard argues, is not believing in nothing, but believing in many things—"too many for the spiritual comfort of blind obedience."¹²

In a world saturated with uncertainty, many of us are more interested in feeling secure than in being free in the fundamental way that Marquard means. We tend to fear losing control or not being able to hold on to things, anxieties that seem to intensify in times of accelerated change and instability. But Eastern traditions remind us that the true nature of things is that we are never in control. We can never hold on to anything. We may accept that idea intellectually, but our panic center continues to be aroused by the idea of letting go.²⁸ Perhaps what we really need is practice, and if so, we should be getting plenty of it from what is described as "the thorough and relentless uncertainization" of the postmodern world.¹² The dissolution of form, the tendency in these times for our cherished worldviews and habits of mind to be continually undermined, may actually be setting us free.

Jean Gebser's recommended alternative to a retreat into fundamentalism was mentioned earlier: to sustain the open quality of the world through our own openness. Buddhist teachings use different language to say something similar when they recommend "staying in the space of uncertainty without trying to reconstruct a reference point."²⁸ For an aikido master, that ongoing kind of openness is accomplished through questioning, through a "spirit of inquiry." What is at the center of this situation (object, event)? What is needed to make it balanced (whole, harmonious)? Asking these kinds of questions of oneself shifts the attention to the present moment and into the place where intuition may arise. It then becomes possible to respond to each instant with precision. [109]

Others have voiced similar ideas about the power of the questioning process to enable each of us to become authentically individual. Hungarian philosopher Georg Kühlewind believes that questioning is an activity of the "I" (the individuality) and can have no other source than this free aspect of the human being:

> What was once *given* as life's meaning institutionally, through the church, social relationships, tradition, is alive today in our ability to *ask*. Whether the fundamental questions are asked or not is a matter of the individual's freedom.[79]

The fundamental questions, the questions of meaning, are not to be asked of so-called experts in the field but posed to oneself. Regardless of how tempting it is to seek certainty elsewhere, the experience of living with one's own fundamental questions is essential for the development of the individuality. No one else, after all, can give *your* answers to those questions.

Each of the artists named in this book practiced, on some level, the spirit of inquiry. For example, the great choreographers of our time, from Isadora Duncan to Twyla Tharp, began their lifework by radically questioning the conventional views of their time. All went to the roots of their art and of themselves to find their own particularity. Duncan, known among dancers as the mother of modern movement, insisted that the dances of no two persons should be alike: "Others began to imitate me, not understanding that it was necessary to go back to a beginning, to find something in themselves first."[150] Martha Graham continued the theme: "There is a vitality, a life force that is translated through you into action. And because there is only one of you in all time, this expression is unique, and if you block it, it will never exist through any other medium and will be lost."[74]

In 1966 Twyla Tharp was at work with her small group in the gym of the Judson Memorial Church, searching for "an honest starting point for ourselves—not in ballet, not in modern dance, but in something absolutely fundamental, something that could honorably be ours. I was getting down to the first building blocks for our dances—before the atom, before the neutron and the proton, down to the quarks, strange and charmed." She goes on:

> We parsed movement into its components, recombining the pieces in various ways. We looked at movement as energy; we looked at it as rhythm; we looked at it up close and far away. We asked, How slow can you go? How fast? ... After five years of performing in silence, I finally let the music play.[151]

Even before Tharp began her own radical inquiry, the original group of choreographers working in the Judson Church gym had ushered in the postmodern era of movement experimentation by questioning every aspect of dance. The group first came together in the fall of 1960, when John Cage asked musician and philosopher Robert Dunn to teach a choreography class at Merce Cunningham's studio. Dunn's repertoire of perspectives already included the worldviews of Buddhism and Taoism as well as those of Heidegger and Sartre "in some personal amalgam." As he tells the story: "I had the notion in teaching of making a 'clearing,' a sort of 'space of nothing,' in which things could appear and grow in their own nature. Before each class I made the attempt to attain this state of mind."[8] His students were encouraged to question everything, from the traditional concert format to the dance aesthetic itself. Improvisation, spontaneous determination, and chance figured large in what has been described as a Zen-like environment.

When Dunn's students decided they needed a place to perform, they came upon the Judson Church, located at the south end of Washington Square in Greenwich Village. From that time, the church became the acknowledged center for avant-garde dance in the city—the Judson Dance Theater. Out of this environment, out of Dunn's "space of nothing," came many of the most respected choreographers of the late-twentieth century, each entirely unique. The more they questioned, it seems, the more individual they became.

None set out to change the world. The Judson group had not consciously tried to create a new artistic culture. Nor had Cage or Cunningham or Duchamp before them. Each simply worked, through questioning, to find the truth of his own individuality, his particular way of sustaining the open quality of the world. And out of that process came artistic change. Zen teachings maintain that if we stop criticizing the culture of our time and focus instead on the practice of remaining in the present moment, "then society and culture will grow out of you."[146]

From this perspective, the dissolution of form can be seen as an opportunity for self-realization. Wherever we turn in today's world, we find ourselves in a "space of uncertainty." The collapse of personal identity markers, the postmodern image of ourselves as simply the "intersections of competing discourses," could be facilitating the traditional spiritual practice of continually releasing whoever and whatever we think we are, in order to meet the next situation clean. Even Virtual Reality may serve to loosen our grip on conventional reality structures, on the cultural conditioning that meditative techniques spend years trying to dismantle.

Finally, if time is accelerating, and with it unpredictable change, the only secure place to be is clearly the present moment. The Zen master advises us to stop longing for some idealized time when everything will be secure and simple: "Life, change, movement, and insecurity are so many names for the same thing."[162] The forms that we see dissolving have never been anything more than patterns of movement, which must flow out — "die" — if the movement is to live, to keep flowing in. In the midst of this ongoing flux, our single certainty is the present moment. How we relate to it is perhaps the only thing that can authentically make a difference, in our own lives and in the life of the world. It is neither necessary nor desirable to choose between beliefs. The meaningful choice is whether we will be open and attentive to life — or not.

Bibliography

1 Abraham, Ralph H. *Chaos, Gaia, Eros.* San Francisco: Harper-Collins, 1994.

2 Alter, Jonathan. "The New Powers That Be." *Newsweek,* January 18, 1999.

3 Anderson, Walter Truett. *Reality Isn't What It Used to Be.* San Francisco: Harper & Row, 1990.

4 ———. *The Truth About the Truth.* New York: G.P. Putnam's Sons, 1995.

5 ———. *The Future of the Self.* New York: Jeremy P. Tarcher/Putnam, 1997.

6 Applebome, Peter. "No Room for Children in a World of Little Adults." *New York Times,* April 26, 1998.

7 Auletta, Ken. "The Microsoft Provocateur." *New Yorker,* May 12, 1997.

8 Banes, Sally. *Democracy's Body: Judson Dance Theater, 1962–1964.* Ann Arbor, Mich.: UMI Research Press, 1983.

9 Bateson, Gregory. *Mind and Nature.* New York: E.P. Dutton, 1979.

10 Baudrillard, Jean. *The System of Objects.* 1968. Reprint, London: Verso, 1996.

11 Bauman, Zygmunt. *Intimations of Postmodernity.* Boston: Routledge, 1992.

12 ———. *Postmodernity and Its Discontents.* New York: New York University Press, 1997.

13 Bell, Daniel. *The Cultural Contradictions of Capitalism.* New York: Basic Books, 1976.

14 Bell, Quentin. *Virginia Woolf: A Biography.* New York: Harcourt Brace Jovanovich, 1972.

15 Berger, Peter. *The Heretical Imperative.* Garden City, N.Y.: Anchor Press/Doubleday, 1979.

16 Berman, Morris. *The Reenchantment of the World.* Ithaca, N.Y.: Cornell University Press, 1981.

17 Berry, Thomas. *The Dream of the Earth.* San Francisco: Sierra Club Books, 1988.

18 Bertens, Hans. *The Idea of the Postmodern.* London: Routledge, 1995.

19 Best, Steven, and Douglas Kellner. *The Postmodern Turn.* New York: Guilford Press, 1997.

20 Bocock, Robert. *Consumption.* London: Routledge, 1993.

21 Bohm, David. *Wholeness and the Implicate Order.* London: Routledge, 1983.

22 Bramwell, Anna. *The Fading of the Greens.* New Haven: Yale University Press, 1994.

23 Briggs, John, and F. David Peat. *Turbulent Mirror.* New York: Harper & Row, 1989.

24 Broder, John M. "The Lewinsky Legacy." *New York Times,* August 2, 1998.

25 Callow, Phillip. *Lost Earth: A Life of Cézanne.* Chicago: Ivan R. Dee, 1995.

26 Campion, Nicholas. *The Great Year: Astrology, Millenarianism, and History in the Western Tradition.* London: Penguin Books, 1994.

27 Cassidy, John. "No Satisfaction." *New Yorker,* January 25, 1999.

28 Chodron, Pema. "News You Can Use." *Shambala Sun,* March 1997.

29 Coan, Richard W. *Human Consciousness and Its Evolution.* Westport, Conn.: Greenwood Press, 1987.

30 Cohen, Selma Jeanne, ed. *Dance as a Theatre Art.* Princeton: Princeton Book, 1974.

31 Combs, Allan. *The Radiance of Being: Complexity, Chaos, and the Evolution of Consciousness.* St. Paul, Minn.: Paragon House, 1995.

32 Cumont, Franz. *The Mysteries of Mithra.* New York: Dover, 1956.

33 Denby, David. "The Contender." *New Yorker,* April 20, 1998.

34 Dunham-Jones, Ellen. "Temporary Contracts: On the Economy of the Post-Industrial Landscape." *Harvard Design Magazine,* Fall 1997.

35 Durning, Alan. *How Much Is Enough? The Consumer Society and the Future of the Earth.* New York: W.W. Norton, 1992.

36 *Economist.* "Spirit of the Age." December 19, 1998.

37 Eddington, Arthur S. *Space, Time, and Gravitation.* Cambridge: Cambridge University Press, 1987.

38 Elgin, Duane. *Awakening Earth.* New York: William Morrow, 1993.

39 Eliot, Jane Winslow. Review of *Fire on the Earth: Anselm Kiefer and the Postmodern World,* by John C. Gilmour. Rudolf Steiner Library Newsletter, Issue 12 & 13. [no date]

40 Eliot, T.S. *The Waste Land and Other Poems.* New York: Harcourt, Brace & World, 1934.

41 Epstein, Joseph. "What to Do About the Arts," in *Dumbing Down,* edited by Katharine Washburn and John Thornton. New York: W.W. Norton, 1996.

42 Everdell, William R. *The First Moderns: Profiles in the Origins of Twentieth-Century Thought.* Chicago: University of Chicago Press, 1997.

43 Feuerstein, Georg. *Structures of Consciousness.* Lower Lake, Calif.: Integral Publishing, 1987.

44 Frank, Thomas C. "Liberation Marketing and the Culture Trust," in *Conglomerates and the Media,* edited by Patricia Aufderheide et al. New York: New Press, 1997.

45 Gebser, Jean. *The Ever-Present Origin.* Athens: Ohio University Press, 1985.

46 Gergen, Kenneth J. *The Saturated Self.* New York: HarperCollins, 1991.

47 Ghose, Aurobindo. *Message of the Gita.* London: G. Allen & Unwin, 1946.

48 Gilmour, John C. *Fire on the Earth: Anselm Kiefer and the Postmodern World.* Philadelphia: Temple University Press, 1990.

49 Gleick, James. *Faster: The Acceleration of Just About Everything.* New York: Pantheon Books, 1999.

50 Goodman, Fred. *The Mansion on the Hill: Dylan, Young, Geffen, Springsteen, and the Head-on Collision of Rock and Commerce.* New York: Random House, 1996.

51 Gopnik, Adam. "The Repressionists." *New Yorker,* July 14, 1997.

52 Greene, Liz. *The Outer Planets and Their Cycles.* Sebastopol, Calif.: CRCS Publications, 1996.

53 Gribbin, John. *Schroedinger's Kittens and the Search for Reality.* New York: Little, Brown, 1995.

54 Grof, Stanislav. *The Adventure of Self-Discovery.* Albany: State University of New York Press, 1988.

55 Grunwald, Henry. "Can the Millennium Deliver?" *Time,* May 11, 1998.

56 Guénon, René. *The Reign of Quantity and the Signs of the Times.* 1945. Reprint, Baltimore: Penguin, 1972.

57 Harmon, Amy. "The Rebel Code." *New York Times,* February 21, 1999.

58 Hassan, Ihab Habib. *The Postmodern Turn.* Columbus: Ohio State University Press, 1987.

59 Herbert, Bob. "Cold Facts of Global Warming." *New York Times,* July 10, 2000.

60 Hertsgaard, Mark. *Earth Odyssey.* New York: Broadway Books, 1999.

61 Hogue, John. *The Millennium Book of Prophecy.* San Francisco: HarperSanFrancisco, 1994.

62 Hollingdale, R.J. *Nietzsche: The Man and His Philosophy.* London: Routledge & Kegan Paul, 1965.

63 Huxtable, Ada Louise. "Living with the Fake, and Liking It." *New York Times,* March 30, 1997.

64 Iggers, Jeremy. *The Garden of Eating: Food, Sex, and the Hunger for Meaning.* New York: Basic Books, 1996.

65 Jameson, Frederic. *Postmodernism or the Cultural Logic of Late Capitalism.* Durham, N.C.: Duke University Press, 1991.

66 Jencks, Charles. *Postmodernism: The New Classicism in Art and Design.* New York: Rizzoli, 1987.

67 Jenkins, Nicholas. "A Life of Beginnings." *New York Times,* January 4, 1998.

68 Johnson, George. "The Unspeakable Things That Particles Do." *New York Times,* July 27, 1997.

69 Kandinsky, Wassily. *Concerning the Spiritual in Art.* 1914. Reprint, New York: Dover Publications, 1947.

70 ——. *Rückblicke (Reminiscences).* 1913. Reprint. In *Complete Writings on Art,* Vol 1. New York: G.K. Hall, 1982.

71 Kaye, Nick. *Postmodernism and Performance.* New York: St. Martin's Press, 1994.

72 Kennedy, Paul. *Preparing for the Twenty-first Century.* Toronto: HarperCollins, 1993.

73 Kingwell, Mark. *Dreams of Millennium: Report from a Culture on the Brink.* Boston: Faber and Faber, 1996.

74 Kornfield, Jack. *A Path with Heart.* New York: Bantam Books, 1993.

75 Korten, David C. *When Corporations Rule the World.* West Hartford, Conn.: Kumarian Press, 1995.

76 Kozinn, Allan. "Music Reconceived as Acoustical Sculpture." *New York Times*, April 13, 1997.

77 Kramer, Eric Mark, and Algis Mickunas. "Gebser's New Understanding." In *Consciousness and Culture: An Introduction to the Thought of Jean Gebser*, edited by Eric Mark Kramer. Westport, Conn.: Greenwood Press, 1992.

78 Kuh, Katharine. *Break-up: The Core of Modern Art.* London: Cory, Adams & Mackay, 1965.

79 Kühlewind, Georg. *From Normal to Healthy: Paths to the Liberation of Consciousness.* Hudson, N.Y.: Lindisfarne Press, 1988.

80 Kumar, Satish. *Path Without Destination.* New York: William Morrow, 1999.

81 Lasalle, Hugo. *Zen: Way to Enlightenment.* 1898. Reprint, London: Burns and Oaks, 1967.

82 Lee, Martyn J. *Consumer Culture Reborn.* London: Routledge, 1993.

83 Lemert, Charles. *Postmodernism Is Not What You Think.* Malden, Mass.: Blackwell Publishers, 1997.

84 Livingston, James. "Schoenberg Breaks with Tonality." In *Great Events from History II.* Vol. 1. Pasadena, Calif.: Salem Press, 1933.

85 Lodziak, Conrad. *Manipulating Needs: Capitalism and Culture.* Boulder, Colo.: Pluto Press, 1995.

86 Lord, M.G. "New Visions of the Cosmos Now That It's Close at Hand." *New York Times,* June 29, 1997.

87 Lovejoy, Margot. *Postmodern Currents: Art and Artists in the Age of Electronic Media.* Upper Saddle River, N. J.: Prentice Hall, 1997.

88 Lovelock, James. *Gaia: A New Look at Life on Earth.* New York: Oxford University Press, 1979.

89 Lyon, David. *Postmodernity.* Minneapolis: University of Minnesota Press, 1994.

90 Lyotard, Jean-Francois. "Answering the Question: What is

Postmodernism?" In *Innovation/Renovation,* edited by Ihab Hassan and Sally Hassan. Madison: University of Wisconsin Press, 1983.

91 MacGregor, Jeff. "More Than Sight Gags and Subversive Satire." *New York Times,* June 20, 1999.

92 Madoff, Steven Henry. "After the Roaring 80's in Art, A Decade of Quieter Voices." *New York Times,* November 2, 1997.

93 ——. "Out of the Ether, a New Continent of Art." *New York Times,* February 14, 1999.

94 Margulis, Lynn, and Dorion Sagan. *What Is Life?* New York: Simon & Schuster, 1995.

95 Marquard, Odo. *In Defense of the Accidental.* New York: Oxford University Press, 1991.

96 Mayer, Jane. "The Inside Scoop." *New Yorker,* September 7, 1998.

97 Mead, Walter Russell. "Asia Devalued." *New York Times,* May 31, 1998.

98 Menand, Louis. "What is 'Art'?" *New Yorker,* February 9, 1998.

99 Michaux, Henri. *Emergences, resurgences.* Geneva: Skira, 1972.

100 Michels, Victoria Kohn. "A Host Who's Silly, Passionate, Gushing and Glad." *New York Times,* June 20, 1999.

101 Moore, Thomas. *Care of the Soul.* New York: HarperCollins, 1992.

102 Muschamp, Herbert. "Blueprint: The Shock of the Familiar." *New York Times Magazine,* December 13, 1998.

103 Newhouse, Victoria. "Designs That Reach Out and Grab." *New York Times,* June 4, 2000.

104 Newman, Judith. "In Sam We Trust." *New York Times,* November 15, 1998.

105 Nietzsche, Friedrich. *Human, All Too Human.* Cambridge: Cambridge University Press, 1986.

106 Oshinsky, David M. "A Nation of Shoppers," *New York Times,* February 21, 1999.

107 Pagels, Heinz. *The Cosmic Code: Quantum Physics as the Language of Nature.* New York: Simon & Schuster, 1982.

108 Pall, Ellen. "Modern Romantic." *New York Times Magazine,* May 11, 1997.

109 Palmer, Wendy. *The Intuitive Body.* Berkeley, Calif.: North Atlantic Books, 1994.

110 Passell, Peter. "When Mega-Mergers Are Mega-Busts." *New York Times,* May 17, 1998.

111 Paul, Hayden. *Revolutionary Spirit.* Shaftesbury, Dorset, England: Element Books, 1989.

112 Peat, F. David. *The Philosophers Stone: Chaos, Synchronicity, and the Hidden Order of the World.* New York: Bantam Books, 1991.

113 Plato. *Timaeus.* Translated by Desmond Lee. New York: Penguin Classics, 1971.

114 Priestley, J.B. *Man and Time.* New York: Dell Publishing, 1968.

115 Purdum, Todd S. "The Way We Are in the Era of Clinton." *New York Times,* March 15, 1998.

116 Renfrew, Colin, and Paul Bahn. *Archaeology.* London: Thames and Hudson, 1991.

117 Rheingold, Howard. *Virtual Reality.* New York: Summit Books, 1991.

118 Rich, Frank. "A Detour in the Theater That No One Predicted." *New York Times,* October 18, 1998.

119 Rosenblum, Robert. *Cubism and Twentieth-Century Art.* New York: Harry N. Abrams. [no date]

120 Ross, Alex. "Visiting Musical Ghosts in Search of Answers." *New York Times,* March 30, 1997.

121 Samuelson, Robert J. "Global Capitalism, R.I.P.?" *Newsweek,* September 14, 1998.

122 Sandler, Irving. *Art of the Postmodern Era.* New York: IconEditions, HarperCollins, 1996.

123 Santillana, G. De, and H. Von Dechend. *Hamlet's Mill.* Gambit, Boston, 1977.

124 Sardello, Robert. *Love and the Soul: Creating a Future for Earth.* New York: HarperCollins, 1995.

125 Schickel, Richard. "Mixed Doubles." *Time,* April 20, 1998.

126 Schiesel, Seth. "The No. 1 Customer: Sorry, It Isn't You." *New York Times,* November 23, 1997.

127 Schjeldahl, Peter. "Art Gavel Comes Down Hard." *Village Voice,* November 17, 1990.

128 ———. "Festivalism." *New Yorker,* July 5, 1999.

129 Settegast, Mary. *Plato, Prehistorian: 10,000 to 5,000 B.C. in Myth and Archaeology.* Cambridge, Mass.: Rotenberg Press, 1986.

130 Sheldrake, Rupert. *A New Science of Life.* Los Angeles: Jeremy Tarcher, 1981.

131 ———. *The Rebirth of Nature.* Rochester, Vt.: Park Street Press, 1991.

132 Siegel, Marcia B. *The Shapes of Change: Images of American Dance.* Boston: Houghton Mifflin, 1979.

133 Sloan, Allen. "The New Rich." *Newsweek,* August 4, 1997.

134 Smith, Roberta. "Galleries Are Labs of a Sort." *New York Times,* February 14, 1999.

135 ———. "Conceptual Art: Over, and Yet Everywhere." *New York Times,* April 25, 1999.

136 Soros, George. *The Crisis of Global Capitalism.* Public Affairs, New York, 1998.

137 Sorrell, Walter, ed. *The Dance Has Many Faces.* Chicago: Chicago Review Press, 1992.

138 Spender, Stephen. *T.S. Eliot.* New York: Viking Press, 1975.

139 Spengler, Oswald. *The Decline of the West.* 2 vols. 1918, 1922. Reprint, New York: Alfred A. Knopf, 1926, 1928.

140 Stavrianos, L.S. *The Promise of the Coming Dark Age.* San Francisco: W.H. Freeman, 1976.

141 Stearns, Peter N. *Millennium III, Century XXI.* Boulder, Colo.: Westview Press, 1996.

142 Stengel, Richard. "Living Large." *New Yorker,* April 27 and May 4, 1998.

143 Strasser, Susan. *Satisfaction Guaranteed: The Making of the American Mass Market.* New York: Pantheon, 1989.

144 Strauss, William, and Neil Howe. *The Fourth Turning.* New York: Broadway Books, 1997.

145 Sutherland, Peter D., and John W. Sewell. "Gather the Nations to Promote Globalization." *New York Times,* February 8, 1998.

146 Suzuki, Shunryu. *Zen Mind, Beginner's Mind.* New York: John Weatherhill, 1970.

147 Szamosi, Geza. *The Twin Dimensions: Inventing Time and Space.* New York: McGraw-Hill, 1986.

148 Talbott, Stephen L. *The Future Does Not Compute.* Sebastopol, Calif.: O'Reilly & Associates, 1995.

149 Tarnas, Richard. *The Passion of the Western Mind.* New York: Harmony Books, 1991.

150 Terry, Walter. *The Dance in America.* New York: Harper & Row, 1956.

151 Tharp, Twyla. *Push Comes to Shove.* New York: Bantam Books, 1992.

152 Thompson, William Irwin. *The American Replacement of Nature.* New York: Doubleday, 1991.

153 [Tomberg, Valentin] *Meditations on the Tarot: A Journey into Christian Hermeticism.* Rockport, Mass.: Element Classics, 1993.

154 Tomkins, Calvin. *Off The Wall: Robert Rauschenberg and the Art World of Our Time.* New York: Doubleday, 1980.

155 ——. *The World of Marcel Duchamp.* New York: Time, Inc., 1966.

156 ——. "Total Abstraction." *New Yorker,* March 25, 1996.

157 *TV Guide,* April 18–24, 1998.

158 Twitchell, James B. *Adcult USA.* New York: Columbia University Press, 1996.

159 Vallier, Dora. *Abstract Art.* New York: Orion Press, 1970.

160 Vitale, Rosanna. "The Significance of Aperspectival Art in Light of Gebser's Work." In *Consciousness and Culture: An Introduction to the Thought of Jean Gebser,* edited by Eric Mark Kramer. Westport, Conn.: Greenwood Press, 1992.

161 Waddington, C.H. *Behind Appearance.* Cambridge: MIT Press, 1970.

162 Watts, Alan. *The Wisdom of Insecurity.* New York: Pantheon, 1951.

163 Wheatley, Margaret. *Leadership and the New Science.* San Francisco: Berrett-Koehler, 1992.

164 Williams, Cynthia J. "Diaghilev's Ballets Russes Astounds Paris." In *Great Events from History,* Vol 1. Pasadena, Calif.: Salem Press, 1933.

165 Wills, Garry. Quoted in *The Postmodern Turn,* by Steven Best and Douglas Kellner. New York: Guilford Press, 1997.

166 Yeats, W.B. "The Second Coming." In *The Collected Poems of W.B. Yeats.* New York: Scribner Paperback Poetry, 1996.

167 Zakaria, Fareed. "Sometimes a Great Nation." *New York Times,* May 18, 1997.

168 ——. "Our Hollow Hegemony: Why Foreign Policy Can't be Left to the Market." *New York Times,* November 1, 1998.

169 Zimmer, Heinrich. *Myths and Symbols in Indian Art and Civilization.* New York: Pantheon Books, 1946.

170 Zohar, Danah. *The Quantum Self.* New York: William Morrow, 1990.

List of Illustrations & Credits

1. Georges Braque, *Piano and Mandola*, Winter 1909–1910. Oil on canvas. c. 36 x 17 inches. Solomon R. Guggenheim Museum. Photograph by Lee B. Ewing. Copyright The Solomon R. Guggenheim Foundation, New York.

2. Pablo Picasso, *Portrait of Daniel-Henry Kahnweiler*, 1910. Oil on canvas, 39 x 28 inches. Art Institute of Chicago: Gift of Mrs. Gilbert W. Chapman in memory of Charles B. Goodspeed, 1948.561. Photograph courtesy of The Art Institute of Chicago.

3. Tom Wesselmann, *Great American Nude #48*, 1963. Oil and collage on canvas, acrylic and collage on board, enameled radiator, table, pot of flowers, window assemblage. 84 x 108 x 34 inches. Kaiser Wilhelm Museum, Krefeld, Germany.

4. David Salle, *Lampwick's Dilemma*, 1989. Oil and acrylic on canvas with insert panels, 94 x 136 inches. Courtesy of Gagosian Gallery, New York.

5. Charles W. Moore, Piazza d'Italia, New Orleans, 1976-1979. Photograph copyright Norman McGrath.

6. Ashley Bickerton, *Tormented Self-Portrait (Susie at Arles)*, 1987–1988. Synthetic polymer paint, bronze powder, and lacquer on wood, anodized aluminum, rubber, plastic, formica, leather, chrome-plated steel, and canvas, 89½ x 68¾ x 15¾ inches. Museum of Modern Art, New York. Purchase. Photograph copyright 2000 The Museum of Modern Art, New York.

7. Richard Hamilton, *Just What Is It That Makes Today's Homes So Different, So Appealing?* 1956. Collage, c. 10 x 10¼ inches. Kunsthalle Tubingen.

8. Barbara Kruger, *Untitled* (I shop therefore I am), 1987. Photographic silkscreen on vinyl, 111 x 113 inches. Private collection. Courtesy Mary Boone Gallery, New York.

9. Andy Warhol, *One Dollar Bill,* 1962. Synthetic polymer paint and silkscreen on canvas, 52 x 72 inches. Copyright The Andy Warhol Foundation for the Visual Arts/Art Resource, New York.

10. Georges Braque, *Castle at La Roche-Guyon,* 1909. Oil on canvas, 36 x 28 inches. Van Abbemuseum, Eindhoven, Holland

11. Paul Cézanne, *Mont Sainte-Victoire,* 1904–1906. Oil on canvas, 28¾ x 36¼ inches. Philadelphia Museum of Art. The George W. Elkins Collection. Photographer, Graydon Wood, 1994.

12. Piet Mondrian, *The Red Tree,* 1908–1909. Oil on canvas, 27½ x 39 inches. Gemeentemuseum, The Hague.

13. Piet Mondrian, *Composition No. 3* (Trees), 1912. Oil on canvas, 37½ x 31½ inches. Gemeentemuseum, The Hague.

14. Piet Mondrian, *Composition With Red, Yellow, Blue and Black,* 1921. Oil on canvas, c. 23½ x 23½ inches. Gemeentemuseum, The Hague.

15. Robert Delaunay, *Champ-de-Mars: The Red Tower,* 1911/1923. Oil on canvas, c. 64 x 51½ inches. Art Institute of Chicago: The Joseph Winterbotham Collection 1959.1. Photograph courtesy of The Art Institute of Chicago.

16. Pablo Picasso, *Man With Violin,* 1911. Oil on canvas, c. 39½ x 30 inches. Philadelphia Museum of Art: Louise and Walter Arensberg Collection.

17. Wassily Kandinsky, *The Red Spot,* 1914. Oil on canvas, 51¼ x 51¼ inches. Musée d'Art Moderne, Centre Pompidou, Paris. Copyright Erich Lessing/Art Resource, New York.

18. Andy Warhol, *Thirty Are Better Than One* (Mona Lisa), 1963. Synthetic polymer paint and silkscreen ink on canvas, 110 x 94½ inches. Copyright The Andy Warhol Foundation/Art Resource, New York.

19. James Rosenquist, *F111,* 1964–1965. Oil on canvas with aluminum, 110 x 94½ inches. Museum of Modern Art, New York. Purchase. Photograph copyright 2000 The Museum of Modern Art, New York.

20. Frank Gehry, The Guggenheim Museum at Bilbao, Spain, 1998. Copyright Jeff Goldberg/Esto.

21. Vincent Van Gogh, *The Starry Night,* 1889. Oil on canvas, 29 x 36¼ inches.

Museum of Modern Art, New York. Acquired through the Lillie P. Bliss Bequest. Photograph copyright 2000 The Museum of Modern Art, New York.

22. Charles Schmidt, *The Firefly: Mariner Nine's Rendezvous with Mars,* Oil on canvas, 24 x 56 inches. Courtesy of the artist and NASA. "Mariner Nine in its historic fly-by of Mars in 1972 revealed for the first time some of the extraordinary geology of the planet including the great valley, Vallis Marinis, shown in the painting."

23. Marcel Duchamp, *Bicycle Wheel,* New York, 1951. (Third version, after lost original of 1913.) Metal wheel mounted on painted wood stool, c. 50½ x 25½ x 16½ inches. Museum of Modern Art, New York: The Sidney and Harriet Janis Collection. Photograph copyright The Museum of Modern Art, New York.

24. James Turrell, *Milk Run II.* Installation in the Kunsthaus Bregenz, Austria, 1997. Courtesy of the artist. Photograph by Gerald Zugman. Copyright James Turrell.

25. Stephen Antonakos, *Walk On Neon,* 1968. Neon, glass, and steel, 10 x 9 x 12 feet. Courtesy of the artist. Copyright Stephen Antonakos.

26. Georges Braque, *Still Life With Tenora* (formerly called *Clarinet*), 1913. Pasted paper, oil, charcoal, chalk, and pencil on canvas, c. 37½ x 47½ inches. Museum of Modern Art, New York: Nelson A. Rockefeller Bequest. Photograph copyright 2000 The Museum of Modern Art, New York.

27. Pablo Picasso, *Portrait of Ambroise Vollard,* 1910. Oil on canvas, c. 36¼ x 25¾ inches. Pushkin State Museum of Fine Arts, Moscow. Scala/Art Resource. Copyright Art Resource, New York.

28. Paul Cézanne, *Still Life with Basket,* 1888–1890. Oil on canvas, 25 x 31 inches. Musee d'Orsay, Paris. Giraudon/Art Resource, New York.

29. Robert Rauschenberg, *Tracer,* 1963. Oil and silkscreen on canvas, c. 84 x 60 inches. Nelson-Atkins Museum of Art, Kansas City, Missouri (Purchase).

30. Daniel Libeskind, "Spiral" Building, side elevation of the original model for the 1996 competition for an extension to The Victoria and Albert Museum, London. Copyright The Victoria and Albert Museum.

31. George Segal, *Portrait of Sidney Janis with Mondrian Painting,* 1967. Plaster figure with Mondrian's *Composition,* 1933, on an easel. Overall: c. 70 x 56¼ x 27¼

inches. Museum of Modern Art, New York: The Sidney and Harriet Janis Collection. Photograph copyright 2000 The Museum of Modern Art, New York.

32. Yves Klein, *Untitled blue monochrome*, 1960. Dry pigment in synthetic resin on canvas on wood, c. 76¾ x 55¼ inches. Staatliche Museen zu Berlin, Preussischer Kulturbesitz, Nationalgalerie. Photocredit: Jorg P. Anders, Berlin, 1978.

Index

High, the, 59, 60, 62

Howe, Neil, 59–63

Humphrey, Doris, 102

implicate order, 48, 126

improvisation, 14, 137

indeterminacy principle, 8, 9, 10, 112, 120

Indonesia, 37

inerrantism, 2

irony, 32, 115

jazz, 92, 118

Johnson, Philip, 13

Joyce, James, 68, 92, 116–117

Judson Dance Theater, 11, 103–104, 136–137

Kali Yuga, 63, 64–65, 79

Kandinsky, Wassily, 7, 69 (fig. 17), 93, 96, 136

Kennedy, John F., 60, 61

Kiefer, Anselm, 78, 120

Klein, Yves, 128 (fig. 32)

Kruger, Barbara, 29 (fig. 8)

Kühlewind, Georg, 129, 134,

Las Vegas, 18

Libeskind, Daniel, 122–23, 125 (fig. 30)

Linux, 100

literalism, 2

literature, 10, 68, 86, 92, 116–117

Lovelock, James, 51, 53, 54–55

Lubovitch, Lars, 104

Madonna, 26

Manvantara, 63, 64, 65, 79

Margulis, Lynn, 51

Marquard, Odo, 132–133

Marx, Karl, 23

mass production, 24

Miami Vice, 37

Michaux, Henri, 107

millenarian, 2, 58

mobile (sculpture), 94

Mona Lisa, 66, 72 (fig. 18), 91

Moholy-Nagy, László, 97

Mondrian, Piet, 45–47 (fig. 12, fig. 13), 49 (fig. 14), 96, 125 (fig. 31), 136

Moore, Charles, 14 (fig. 5)

morphic resonance, 49–50

Morris, Mark, 104

movies, 37, 73, 74, 77

Moynihan, Daniel Patrick, 83

music, 37

    classical, 14, 68, 73, 78

    jazz, 92, 118

    modern, 68, 92, 118

    postmodern, 14

    ragtime, 92, 118

    rock, 33

    MTV, 14, 16

Myhrwold, Nathan, 76

Native American history, 32
neon, 14, 97
New Age, 2, 20, 61, 102
niche groups, 61–62
Nichols, Mike, 73
Nietzsche, Friedrich, 130–131
Nikolais, Alwin, 103
Nijinsky, Vaslav, 68
nostalgia, 78, 104–105

obsolescence, 35–36

Pagels, Heinz, 129
Paik, Nam June, 119
Persian Empire, 82
photography, multiple exposure in, 116
physics, 8–9, 42, 66, 115
Picasso, Pablo, 6 (fig. 2), 21, 43, 66, 67
    (fig. 16), 92, 93, 106 (fig. 27), 116,
    136
Pisces, age of, 80, 85–89, 131
    principles of, 86–89, 104–105
Plato, 52, 126
Platonic Year, 80
population, world, 54
postmodern, 133
    art, 12 (fig. 4), 13, 101–102, 125–126
    architecture, 13, 15 (fig. 5)
    dance, 14, 102–104, 135–137

defined, 10, 119
    literature, 10, 13
    music, 14
    precession of the equinoxes, 80
Priestley, J.B., 113, 131
Psycho, 79
Pynchon, Thomas, 102

quantum theory, 8, 48, 88, 93, 115, 129

ragtime, 92, 118
Rauschenberg, Robert, 103, 120, 121
    (fig. 29)
"readymades," 66, 94, 95 (fig. 23)
recycling, cultural, 79
refugees, 58
Reich, Steve, 102
"reign of quantity," 70–76, 107, 131
Renfrew, Colin, 57
Rilke, Rainer Maria, 41
Rome, 82, 83
Rosenquist, James, 74–75 (fig. 19)

Salle, David, 12 (fig. 4)
Sardello, Robert, 52–53
Schjeldahl, Peter, 75
Schoenberg, Arnold, 68, 92, 118
Schmidt, Charles, 88 (fig. 22)
Segal, George, 125 (fig. 31
Seinfeld, 37
Sheldrake, Rupert, 48–50

The typeface for the text of *Mona Lisa's Moustache* is Stempel Garamond, set 11 point with 14 points of leading; it was issued by the Stempel foundry in 1924 and is now available through the digital library of Linotype. It is the only modern Garamond type family to have both the roman and italic based on the original High Renaissance fonts cut by French type designer, Claude Garamond, born 1480.

Text design & composition by
Scott L. Perrizo at
CROSSINGS PRESS, *typographers*

An Alexandria Book

PHANES PRESS publishes quality books on
philosophy, mythology, ancient religions, the
humanities, cosmology, and culture. To receive a
copy of our catalogue, write:

Phanes Press
PO Box 6114
Grand Rapids, MI 49516
USA

www.phanes.com

DATE DUE

GAYLORD			PRINTED IN U.S.A.